HANDY REFERENCE

WordPro

Ctrl+F .... Launches Find & Replace
Ctrl+G .... Launches the Go To dialog
Ctrl+E .... Centres text
Ctrl+L .... Left-justifies text
Ctrl+R .... Right-justifies text
Ctrl+J .... Applies full (left and right) justification
Ctrl+Shift+Z or Alt+Shift+Backspace .. Redoes the last action
Ctrl+N .... Restores text formatting to normal
Ctrl+W .... Word-underlines text (or removes word underlining)
Ctrl+F2 .... Launches a spell check

1-2-3

F2 .... Launches Edit Mode
Ctrl+F .... Launches a find or find-and-replace operation
Ctrl+F2 .... Launches a spell-check
Ctrl+N .... Restores data formatting to normal
Ctrl+Home .... Moves to first cell
Ctrl+Pg Up ..... Moves to next worksheet
Ctrl+Pg Down .... Moves to previous worksheet

Approach

Ctrl+B ....
Ctrl+D ....
Ctrl+Home (in Browse) ... Moves to first record
Ctrl+End (in Browse) .... Moves to final record
Ctrl+W .... Launches Go To Record dialog
Ctrl+Shift+B ..... Launches Print Preview
Ctrl+Shift+D .... Inserts current date
Page Down (in forms) .... Next record
Page Up (in forms) .... Previous record
Ctrl+Up Cursor (in forms in Design mode) .... Zooms In
Ctrl+Down Cursor (in forms in Design mode) .... Zooms Out
Ctrl+1 (in forms in Design mode) .... Zooms to 100% View

Freelance Graphics

Ctrl+W .... Closes the active file
Ctrl+G .... Launches the Go To Page dialog (but not in Outliner view)
F9 .... Redraws the screen
Alt+F9 .... Alternates between displaying in colour and black-and-white
F7 .... Launches the New Page dialog

SmartSuite as a whole

Ctrl+O ....Opens an existing file
Ctrl+S .... Saves the active document
Ctrl+P .... Prints the active document
Ctrl+B .... Emboldens or removes emboldening (but not in Approach)
Ctrl+I ....Italicises or removes italicisation (but not in Approach)
Ctrl+U .... Underlines or removes underlining (but not in Approach)
Ctrl+Z or Alt+Backspace ....Undoes the last action

ABOUT THE SERIES

In easy steps series is developed for time-sensitive people who want results fast. It is designed for quick, easy and effortless learning.

By using the best authors in the field, combined with our in-house expertise in computing, this series is ideal for all computer users. It explains the essentials simply, concisely and clearly - without the unnecessary verbal blurb. We strive to ensure that each book is technically superior, effective for easy learning and offers the best value.

Learn the essentials **in easy steps** - accept no substitutes!

Titles in the series include:

Operating Systems
Windows 95	1-874029-28-8

Applications - Integrated
Microsoft Office	1-874029-37-7
Microsoft Office 97	1-874029-66-0
Microsoft Works	1-874029-41-5
SmartSuite (97)	1-874029-67-9

Applications - General
Access	1-874029-57-1
Excel	1-874029-69-5
PowerPoint	1-874029-63-6
Word	1-874029-39-3
Word 97	1-874029-68-7
WordPerfect	1-874029-59-8

Accounting and Finance
Microsoft Money UK	1-874029-61-X
Quicken UK	1-874029-71-7
Sage Instant Accounting	1-874029-44-X
Sage Sterling for Windows	1-874029-43-1

Internet
CompuServe UK	1-874029-33-4
FrontPage	1-874029-60-1
HTML	1-874029-46-6
Internet Explorer	1-874029-58-X
Internet UK	1-874029-73-3
Netscape Navigator	1-874029-47-4

Graphics and Desktop Publishing
CorelDRAW	1-874029-72-5
PageMaker	1-874029-35-0
PagePlus	1-874029-49-0
Publisher	1-874029-56-3

Development Tools
Visual Basic	1-874029-74-1
Visual J++	1-874029-75-X

Hardware
Upgrading Your PC	1-874029-76-8

For credit card sales and volume discounts Tel: 01926 817999 or EMail: sales@computerstep.com

For international orders and rights Fax: +44 1926 817005 or EMail: sevanti@computerstep.com

EMail your reader comments to: harshad@computerstep.com

Visit our web site at http://www.computerstep.com

SMARTSUITE
in easy steps

Stephen Copestake

In easy steps is an imprint of Computer Step
Southfield Road . Southam
Warwickshire CV33 OFB . England

Tel: 01926 817999 Fax: 01926 817005
http://www.computerstep.com

Second edition published 1997
First published 1996
Copyright © 1996-97 by Computer Step

Notice of Liability
Every effort has been made to ensure that this book contains accurate
and current information. However, Computer Step and the author
shall not be liable for any loss or damage suffered by readers as a
result of any information contained herein.

Trademarks
Microsoft and Windows are registered trademarks of Microsoft
Corporation. SmartSuite, WordPro, 1-2-3, Approach and Freelance
Graphics are registered trademarks of Lotus Development
Corporation. All other trademarks are acknowledged as belonging to
their respective companies.

Printed and bound in the United Kingdom

ISBN 1-874029-67-9

Contents

4. Approach 101

Common Features

This chapter shows you how SmartSuite provides a common look, so you can get started quickly in any module. You'll learn how to create new documents and open/save existing ones, both locally and on the Internet. You'll also learn how to use SmartMasters and SmartCenter.

Covers

Introduction (1)

Lotus SmartSuite consists of four principal modules:

- WordPro (word processor)

- 1-2-3 (spreadsheet)

- Approach (database)

- Freelance Graphics (slide show creator)

SmartSuite also provides further modules. However, these are outside the scope of this book. Any reference to 'SmartSuite modules' therefore refers solely to WordPro, 1-2-3, Approach & Freelance Graphics.

All four modules provide a high level of functionality and ease of use. Another advantage of SmartSuite is that the four modules, despite being market leaders in their own right, are well integrated. To a large extent, they share a common look and feel.

The illustration below shows the WordPro opening screen. Flagged are components which are common to the other modules, too.

SmartIcons provide instant access to commonly used SmartSuite features. Available SmartIcons vary slightly from module to module.

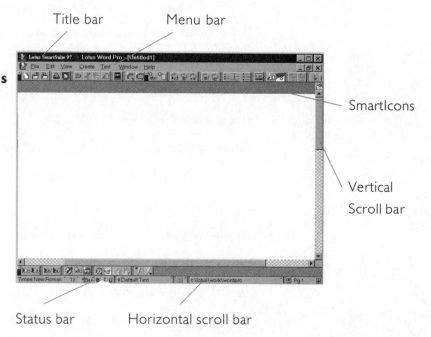

Title bar   Menu bar

SmartIcons

Vertical Scroll bar

Status bar   Horizontal scroll bar

Introduction (2)

Compare this with the following:

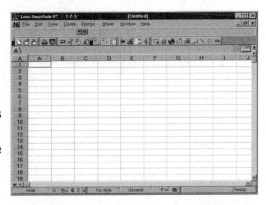

1-2-3 screen

Notice the screen components that are held in common. The purpose of this shared approach is to ensure that users of SmartSuite can move between modules with the minimum of readjustment.

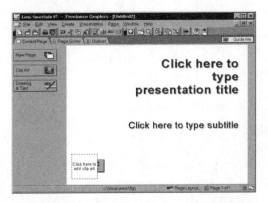

Freelance Graphics screen

There are, of course, differences between the module screens; we'll explore these in later sections.

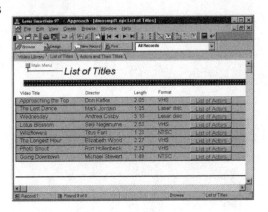

Approach screen

SmartIcons (1)

'Cycling' is a feature unique to SmartSuite. When you click a Cycle button repeatedly, SmartSuite steps through associated options automatically until the correct one is activated.

All four principal SmartSuite modules provide access to a variety of SmartIcons. These are buttons you can click to initiate editing actions, and are contained in an on-screen bar which varies according to module. SmartIcons symbolise and allow easy access to often-used commands which would normally have to be invoked via one or more menus.

For example, WordPro's default SmartIcon bar lets you:

- create, open, save and print documents

- launch Infoboxes (see later in this section)

- cycle through alignment and/or indent options

- cycle through typeface and/or type size options

- cycle through text attribute options (bold, italic and underline)

- spell-check text

by simply clicking on the relevant button.

Hiding/revealing SmartIcons - the menu route
In WordPro, pull down the View menu. Do the following:

In Freelance Graphics, 1-2-3 and Approach, pull down the View menu and click Show SmartIcons. Repeat to hide SmartIcons.

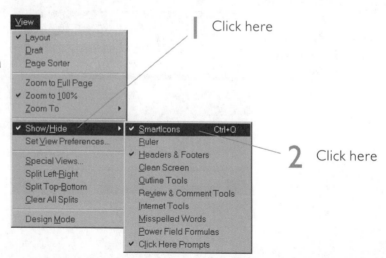

SmartIcons (2)

Hiding/revealing SmartIcons - an alternative

You can use another, and more versatile method to control which SmartIcon sets (bars) display. (Just about any editing operation you can perform from within SmartSuite menus can be incorporated as a SmartIcon, for ease of access.) Using this method, you can hide a specific set, or all sets.

In any module, do the following:

Click any SmartIcon command button, as here

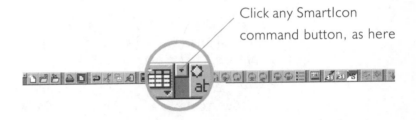

Now do either of the following:

REMEMBER

The options here vary according to the module you're currently using.

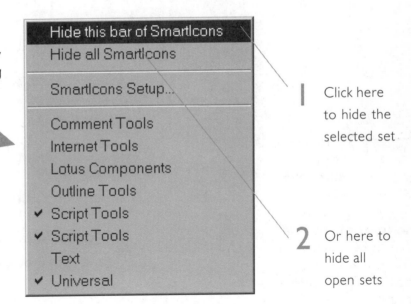

Click here to hide the selected set

Or here to hide all open sets

SmartIcons (3)

Customising SmartIcons

You can:

- specify which bar displays

- add buttons to existing SmartIcon bars

- remove buttons from bars

- specify button size

In any module, click a SmartIcon command button (see SmartIcons (2) for how to do this). In the menu that appears, click SmartIcon Setup.

Now carry out step 1 below to specify which bar displays. Follow step 2 to add a button to the bar, or step 3 to remove an existing one. Finally, carry out step 4.

3 Click a button; drag it off the bar

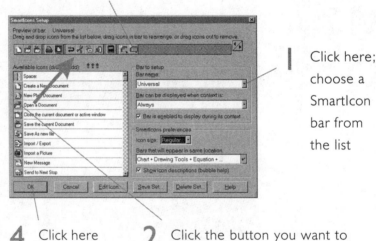

I Click here; choose a SmartIcon bar from the list

HANDY TIP

To adjust the size of SmartIcon buttons, click the arrow to the right of the Icon Size field; select the size you want from the list. Then follow step 4.

4 Click here

2 Click the button you want to add; drag it onto the bar *in the dialog*

Infoboxes - an overview

SmartSuite modules offer a feature which, until now, has only been seen in top-of-the-range Desktop Publishing packages. You can use *Infoboxes,* collections of linked formatting features (called 'properties' in SmartSuite), to make editing changes.

Below is the Text Properties Infobox from WordPro:

To activate a different Infobox, click here; select the new Infobox from the list

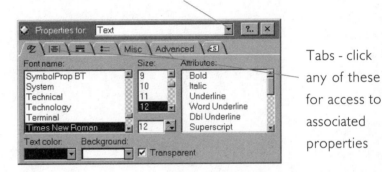

Tabs - click any of these for access to associated properties

Infoboxes provide the following advantages:

- If you want, you can have them stay open on-screen while you work (unlike dialogs, which close when you've finished with them). In this way, you can easily make multiple changes with the minimum of effort.

- You can use standard Windows techniques to move them to new locations on-screen.

- Changes you make within an Infobox are applied automatically, while you watch. In effect, this is a Preview facility.

The following are some of the areas where Infoboxes are useful: text formatting, page layout, working with frames, working with headers/footers, columns and drawings.

Launching Infoboxes

SmartSuite lets you use SmartIcons to launch Infoboxes.

Approach and Freelance Graphics

 This is an excerpt from the default Freelance Graphics SmartIcon bar; the Infobox icon, however, is identical in both Freelance Graphics and Approach.

The various modules employ slightly different techniques. In Approach and Freelance Graphics, first select whatever it is you want to change. Then do the following:

Click here to launch the relevant Infobox

WordPro and 1-2-3

WordPro and 1-2-3, on the other hand, use a more individualistic approach. For examples of this, look at the SmartIcon section below:

SmartIcon which launches the Range Infobox

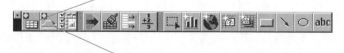

SmartIcon which launches the Sheet Infobox

 This example is the icon which launches the Text Properties Infobox from WordPro. It's used to change typographical features.

The point here is that WordPro and 1-2-3 provide a variety of *specific* Infobox icons. Each contains a yellow star on a grey background.

Yellow star

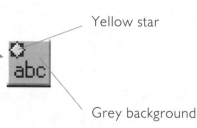

Grey background

New document creation

All SmartSuite modules let you:

- create new blank documents

- create new documents based on automated templates called SmartMasters

Creating blank documents is the simplest route to new document creation; use this if you want to define the document components yourself from scratch. This is often not the most efficient way to create new documents.

SmartMasters are special templates (document models containing pre-assigned formatting and/or text) which provide a shortcut to the creation of new documents. When activated, SmartMasters are often organised with preset divider tabs, and contain special 'click here' blocks which tell you where to insert relevant text. SmartMasters greatly simplify and speed up the creation of new documents while at the same time producing highly professional results.

Documents created with the use of SmartMasters can easily be amended subsequently.

The illustration below shows the Newsletter SmartMaster which comes with WordPro.

Preset divider tab

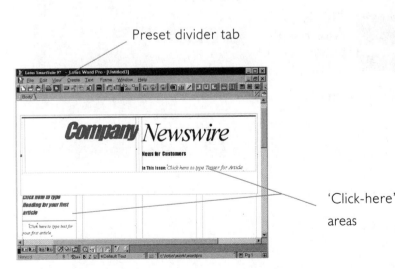

'Click-here' areas

Creating blank documents (1)

You can create a new blank document from within any of the SmartSuite modules. However, the procedures are slightly different.

A version of the New dialog (called the 'Welcome' screen) also launches automatically whenever you launch a module.

In WordPro and Approach

Pull down the File menu. Click New Document in WordPro or New Database in Approach. Now carry out the following steps, as appropriate:

This is WordPro's New Document dialog.

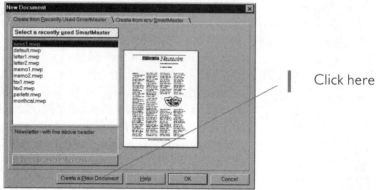

Click here

This is Approach's New dialog.

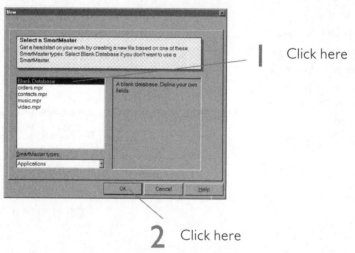

Click here

2 Click here

16   **SmartSuite in easy steps**

Creating blank documents (2)

In 1-2-3 and Freelance Graphics

Pull down the File menu. Now click New Workbook in 1-2-3 or New Presentation in Freelance Graphics. Do the following, as appropriate:

 This is 1-2-3's New Workbook dialog.

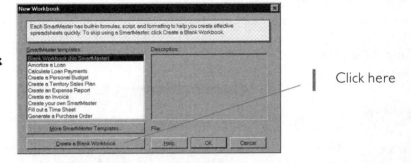

Click here

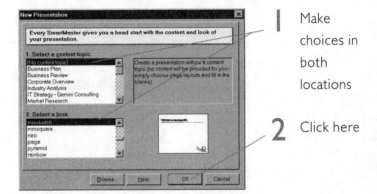

Make choices in both locations

2 Click here

 **Freelance Graphics uses two dialogs. Complete steps 1-4.**

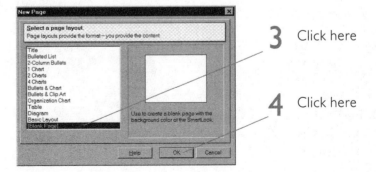

3 Click here

4 Click here

Using SmartMasters (1)

SmartSuite provides a large number of SmartMasters. With these, you can create a wide variety of professional-quality documents. For example, you can create newsletters, business plans and reviews, faxes, financial statements, letters, invoices, payment schedules, memos, reports...

For another way to create new documents based on SmartMasters, see the 'Working with SmartCenter' topic later.

In WordPro and Approach

Pull down the File menu. Click New Document in WordPro or New Database in Approach. Now do the following:

This is WordPro's New Document dialog.

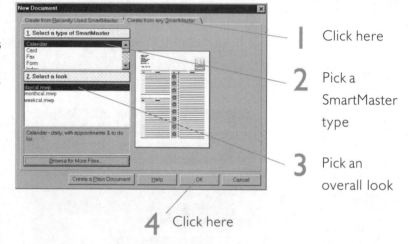

I Click here

2 Pick a SmartMaster type

3 Pick an overall look

4 Click here

This is the Approach version of the New dialog.

To use a template – a simplified SmartMaster – click here: choose Templates in the list. Now follow steps 1 & 2.

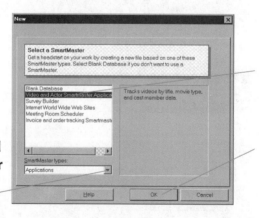

I Pick a database model

2 Click here

Using SmartMasters (2)

In 1-2-3 and Freelance Graphics

Pull down the File menu. Now click New Workbook in 1-2-3 or New Presentation in Freelance Graphics. Carry out the following steps, as appropriate:

 This is 1-2-3's New File dialog.

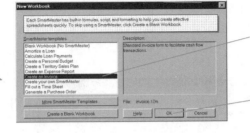

1 Pick a SmartMaster type

2 Click here

 Freelance Graphics uses two dialogs. Complete steps 1-4.

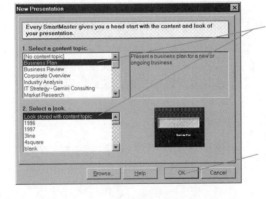

1 Make choices in both locations

2 Click here

 Content topics help you create effective slide shows by suggesting suitable text and graphics, when appropriate.

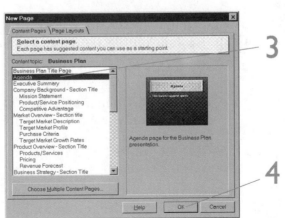

3 Pick a Content topic

4 Click here

Opening files

You can open WordPro, 1-2-3, Approach and Freelance Graphics documents you've already created.

In any module, pull down the File menu and click Open. Now carry out the following steps, as appropriate:

2 Click here. In the drop-down list, click the drive which hosts the file

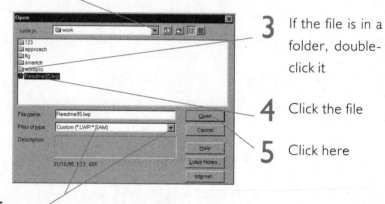

3 If the file is in a folder, double-click it

4 Click the file

5 Click here

HANDY TIP **You can also use the Documents section available from the Windows Start menu to open recently used SmartSuite files – see your Windows documentation for how to do this.**

1 Make sure the relevant file type is shown. If it isn't, click the arrow and select it from the drop-down list

The Open dialogs for the WordPro, 1-2-3, Freelance Graphics and Approach modules vary slightly. For instance:

• the Files of type field lists differing file formats

• in the 1-2-3 Open dialog, you can opt to open the file on a 'read only' basis (where no amendments to the document can be saved to disk).

Opening files from the Internet

In any module, you can open documents directly from the World Wide Web or FTP servers.

 Re step 3 –
people
accessing
the Web
from a company
network are
particularly liable to
need to use a proxy
server.

Web connections

Pull down the File menu and click Internet, Open from Internet. Now carry out the following steps, as appropriate:

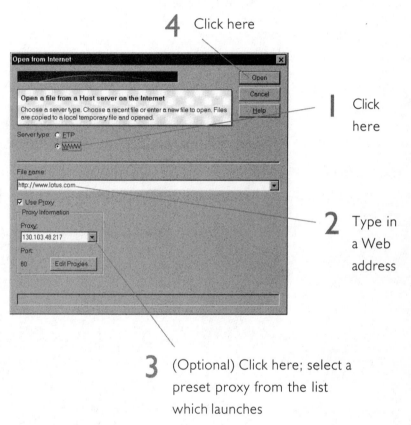

4 Click here

| Click
here

2 Type in
a Web
address

3 (Optional) Click here; select a
preset proxy from the list
which launches

 Before you
open a FTP
file, you
need to set
up your host
connection. To do
this in any module,
pull down the File
menu and click
Internet, FTP
Connection Setup.
Complete the dialog
which launches – if
you need any help
doing this (or with
any other aspect of
connection) consult
your provider, or
buy *Internet UK in*
easy steps.
Finally, click OK
in the FTP
Connection Setup
dialog.

FTP Connections

The above procedures establish a World Wide Web connection. To make a FTP connection instead, click FTP in step 1. Then complete the dialog as necessary (for help with this, see page 20). Finally, follow step 4 to open the selected FTP archive/file.

Saving files

It's important to save your work at frequent intervals, in order to avoid data loss in the event of a hardware fault or power interruption. SmartSuite uses a consistent approach to saving.

Saving a document for the first time

In any of the modules, pull down the File menu and click Save or Save As. Now do the following:

Click here. In the drop-down list, click the drive you want to host the document

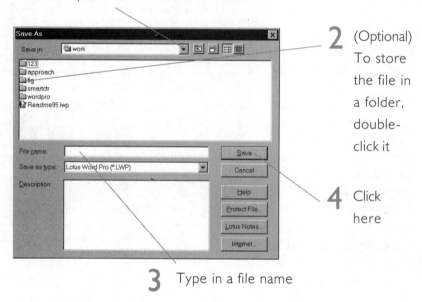

2 (Optional) To store the file in a folder, double-click it

4 Click here

3 Type in a file name

Saving previously saved documents

In any of the modules, pull down the File menu. Now:

- In WordPro, Freelance Graphics or 1-2-3, click Save.

- In Approach, click Save Approach File.

No dialog launches; instead, SmartSuite saves the latest version of your document to disk, overwriting the previous version.

Saving files to the Internet

You can save files in all four modules to a FTP server.

Launch the Save As dialog – for how to do this, see the 'Saving files' topic on page 22. Then do the following:

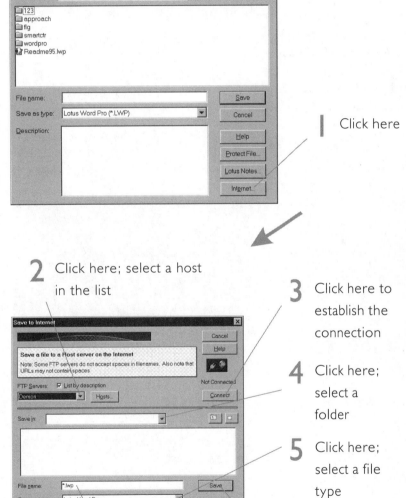

Before you save a file to a FTP server, you need to set up your host connection. To do this in any module, pull down the File menu and click Internet, FTP Connection Setup. Complete the dialog which launches – if you need any help doing this (or with any other aspect of connection) consult your provider, or buy *Internet UK in easy steps*.

Finally, click OK in the FTP Connection Setup dialog.

1   Click here

2   Click here; select a host in the list

3   Click here to establish the connection

4   Click here; select a folder

5   Click here; select a file type

6   Type in a name

7   Click here

Publishing to the Internet

HANDY TIP

After step 4, the HTML Import/ Export Options dialog may launch. If it does, complete it as necessary. Then click OK. Now follow the next procedure...

All four modules allow you to export files to HTML (Hypertext Mark-up Language) format. These can then be placed on a FTP server.

Launch the Save As dialog – for how to do this, see the 'Saving a document for the first time' topic on page 22. Then carry out steps 1 and 2. Now refer to the Save as type field and do the following:

Click here; select HTML (*.HTM) in the list

Now carry out steps 3 and 4 on page 22. Finally, pull down the File menu and click Internet, Publish as Web Page(s), then carry out the following steps:

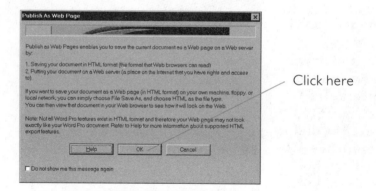

Click here

The Save to Internet dialog now launches. For how to complete this, see page 23 – carry out steps 2-4 and 6-7 (you should omit 5 because SmartSuite preselects HTML automatically).

SmartCenter - an overview

SmartSuite comes with a unique command centre, SmartCenter. Among other things, you can use this to:

- run SmartSuite programs

- create new documents based on SmartMasters

- launch a desktop calendar and address book

- launch Internet connections

SmartCenter uses a filing cabinet analogy.

Customising SmartCenter

By default, SmartCenter displays near the Windows Task bar. However, if you want you can have it at the top of your screen. You can also arrange to hide it until wanted (by default, it displays on screen continuously). Carry out the following steps, as appropriate:

Click here

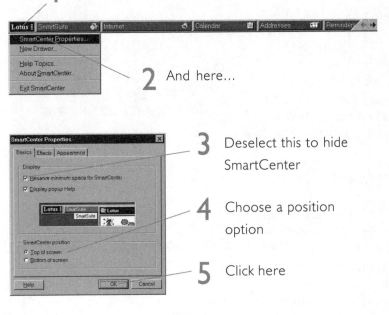

2 And here...

HANDY TIP

Re step 3 - during normal editing, move the mouse pointer to the top or bottom of the screen (as appropriate - see step 4) and click once to make SmartCenter visible. To hide it again, click anywhere outside it.

3 Deselect this to hide SmartCenter

4 Choose a position option

5 Click here

Working with SmartCenter

Activating drawers

To activate a SmartCenter drawer, move the mouse pointer over it – see the illustration below.

Then click once. The next illustration shows four of the main SmartCenter drawers activated. Follow the instructions to use them.

To launch a preset Internet connection, click the appropriate heading in the Internet drawer. Then follow the on-screen instructions.

Double-click a program's icon to launch it

To enter a name/address, click a letter. Right-click; in the menu, click Add Name and Address. Complete the dialog; click OK

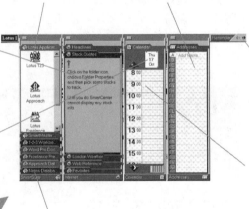

Click the arrow to view further drawers

Click this to change the day in the Calendar drawer. In the calendar that launches, click the required date.

To enter an appointment, click the relevant slot; type in details in the Create Appointment dialog and click OK

To open an existing document, click the appropriate tab, then double-click the relevant icon

To create a new document based on a SmartMaster, click the SmartMaster tab in the SmartSuite drawer; double-click the relevant icon.

Closing drawers

To close a drawer, click once on the base.

WordPro

This chapter gives you the basics of using WordPro. You'll learn how to enter text and negotiate the WordPro screen. You'll also discover how to format text and create/apply text styles. Finally, you'll learn to insert pictures and then customise page layout/printing.

Covers

The WordPro screen

Below is an illustration of the WordPro screen.

The Status bar displays information relating to the active document (e.g. what page you're on, the current typeface/ type size and the date/time).

Title bar   Menu bar

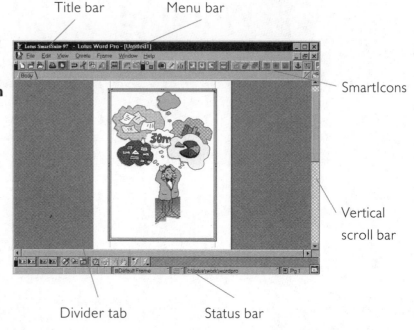

SmartIcons

Vertical scroll bar

Divider tab   Status bar

The 4 **in the menu signifies** that the item is currently visible.

Some of these – e.g. the scroll bars – are standard to just about all programs which run under Windows. A few of them can be hidden, if required.

Specifying which screen components display

Pull down the View menu. Then do the following:

Re step 2 - click Clean Screen to hide all extraneous screen components (this increases working space). To return to normal editing, click [ ] in the bottom right-hand corner of the screen.

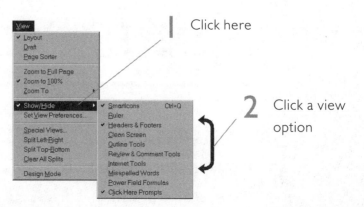

Click here

2 Click a view option

Entering text

WordPro lets you enter text as soon as you're presented with the basic editing screen. You enter text at the insertion point:

The text insertion point

WordPro has automatic word wrap. This means that you don't have to press Return to enter text on a new line; a new line is automatically started for you, when required. Only press Return if you need to begin a new paragraph.

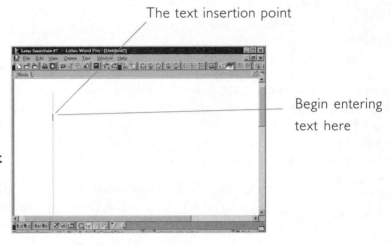

Begin entering text here

Special characters

Most of the text you need to enter can be typed in directly from the keyboard. However, it's sometimes necessary to enter special characters (e.g. bullets like ☞, or ©). WordPro lets you do this directly.

Place the insertion point at the correct location. Pull down the File menu and click Text, Insert Other. Do the following:

1 Click here; select a font from the list

2 Double-click a character

3 Click here

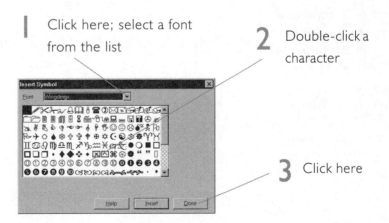

Moving around in documents (1)

REMEMBER

The following useful keystroke combinations are unique to WordPro. To move from an Infobox to the open document (& vice versa), hit:
Alt+Enter
To the start of the next sentence:
Ctrl+.
To the start of the previous sentence:
Ctrl+,
To the start of the next paragraph:
Ctrl+↓
To the start of the current paragraph:
Ctrl+↑

HANDY TIP

When you drag the box on the Vertical Scroll bar, SmartSuite displays an indicator showing which page and section you're up to.

You can use the following to move through WordPro documents:

- keystrokes

- the vertical/horizontal scroll bars

- the Go To dialog

Using keystrokes

SmartSuite implements the standard Windows direction keys. Use the left, right, up and down cursor keys in the usual way. Additionally, Home, End, Page Up and Page Down work normally.

Using the scroll bars

Use your mouse to perform any of the following actions:

Click anywhere here to jump to the left or right

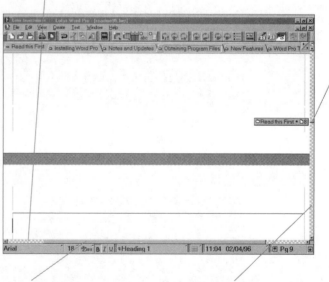

Drag this up or down to move through the active document

Drag this to the left or right to extend the viewing area

Click anywhere here to jump to another location in the document

Moving around in documents (2)

Using the Go To dialog

You can use the Go To dialog to navigate through the open document.

Pull down the Edit menu and click Go To. Now do the following:

You can use a keyboard shortcut to launch the Go To dialog: simply press Ctrl+G.

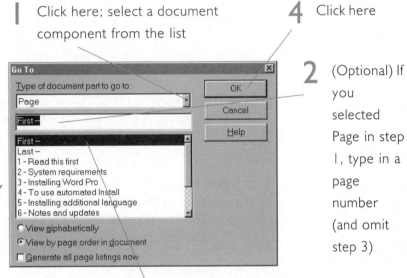

1 Click here; select a document component from the list

4 Click here

2 (Optional) If you selected Page in step 1, type in a page number (and omit step 3)

3 Click First or Last, to determine direction of movement

Re step 2 – you can use an alternative technique to move to a specific page. Click any character-based page definition (see 'Refinements...' for more information). Then carry out step 4 after omitting step 3.

Refinements...

SmartSuite automatically creates definitions of each page within a document by noting the first few characters. As a result, if you select Page in step 1 above, you can opt to move to a specific page *based on recognition of the contents* – see the Remember Tip in the margin for how to do this.

By default, SmartSuite arranges these potted page descriptions in page order. If you want them organised in alphabetical order instead, click View Alphabetically in the dialog above.

Document views - an overview

WordPro lets you examine your work in various ways, according to the approach you need. It calls these 'views'.

There are three principal views:

Draft
Draft View is used for basic text editing. In Draft View, most formatting elements are still visible; for instance, coloured, emboldened or italicised text displays faithfully. On the other hand, page breaks and headers/footers aren't shown. Certain kinds of inserted pictures display faithfully; others don't.

For these reasons, Draft View is quick and easy to use. It's suitable for bulk text entry and editing. It may not be suitable for use with graphics (for this, switch to Layout view – see below).

Layout
Layout view – the default – works like Draft view, with one exception: it's fully WYSIWYG (What You See Is What You Get), and the positioning of all items on the page is reproduced accurately. What you see is an accurate representation of what your document will look like when printed. Headers and footers are visible, and can be edited directly; margins display faithfully; and all pictures occupy their correct position on-screen.

In Layout view, the screen is updated more slowly. As a result, use it when your document is nearing completion, for final proofing. This suggestion is particularly apt if you're working with a slow computer.

Page Sorter
Page Sorter view is another new SmartSuite feature 'borrowed' from high-end Desktop Publishing programs. In Page Sorter view, documents are shown as 'thumbnails' representing individual pages (based on sections and page breaks).

Using views

The view that is currently active has a ✓ against it.

Switching between views

Pull down the View menu. Click Draft, Layout or Page Sorter, as appropriate.

Using Page Sorter

In Page Sorter, you can:

* expand or contract groups of pages

* visually move pages or groups of pages

When you've launched Page Sorter, carry out step 1 below to move a page or page group. Or follow step 2 to expand or contract a group.

You can edit text in the normal way within Page Sorter view.

Click a page's title bar; drag it to a new location (the cursor becomes a page icon). Release the mouse button to confirm the move.

Re step 2 – the circle shows a magnified view of the expand/contract control button. If – (rather than +) displays, clicking it contracts the group.

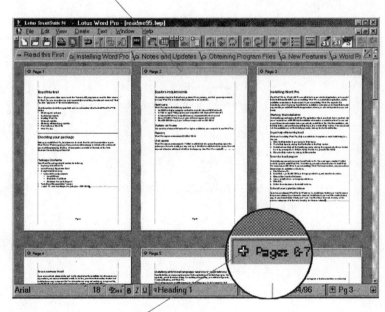

2 Click here to expand a page group

Changing zoom levels

The ability to vary the level of magnification for the active WordPro document is often useful. Sometimes, it's helpful to 'zoom out' (i.e. decrease the magnification) so that you can take an overview; at other times, you'll need to 'zoom in' (increase the magnification) to work in greater detail. WordPro lets you do either of these very easily.

You can do any of the following:

- choose from preset zoom levels (e.g. 100%, 75%)

- specify your own zoom percentage

- choose a zoom setting excluding document margins

Setting the zoom level

Pull down the View menu. Carry out step 1 below. Then, to apply a preset zoom percentage, follow step 2. Or follow steps 3-5 inclusive to customise the zoom level.

HANDY TIP

Click Zoom to Full Page to have an entire page display.

Click here

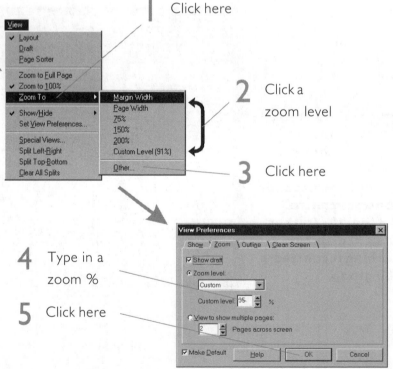

2 Click a zoom level

3 Click here

4 Type in a zoom %

5 Click here

Formatting text - an overview

WordPro lets you format text in a variety of ways. Very broadly, however, and for the sake of convenience, text formatting can be divided into two overall categories:

Character formatting

Character formatting is concerned with altering the *appearance* of selected characters. Examples include:

- changing the font

- changing the type size

- colouring text

- changing the font attributes (bold, italic, underlining etc.)

- superscripting and subscripting text

 The distinction between character and paragraph formatting is sometimes blurred: for instance, both can relate to font appearance. When it comes to text styles, however, there is less confusion (see later topics for how to use styles).

Character formatting is a misnomer in one sense: it can also be applied to specified paragraphs of text, or to parts of specified paragraphs.

Paragraph formatting

Paragraph formatting has to do with the structuring and layout (as well as the appearance) of one or more paragraphs of text.

Examples include:

- specifying paragraph indents/tabs

- specifying paragraph alignment (e.g. left or right justification)

- specifying paragraph and line spacing

- imposing borders and/or fills on paragraphs

- applying typefaces and type sizes

- colouring text

Changing the font and/or type size

Character formatting can be changed in two principal ways:

- from within the Text Properties Infobox
- (to a lesser extent) by using 'cycling'

HANDY TIP

SmartSuite uses standard Windows procedures for text selection.

Applying a new font or type size (1)

First, select the text whose typeface and/or type size you want to amend. Pull down the Text menu and click Text Properties. Now carry out step 1 and/or 2 below:

Click the font you want to use

HANDY TIP

Re step 2 - as well as whole point sizes, you can also enter fractions (to 3 decimal places). For instance, WordPro will accept 10, 10.6 or 10.879... This level of precision - until now, unknown in a word processor - is another feature borrowed from DTP packages.

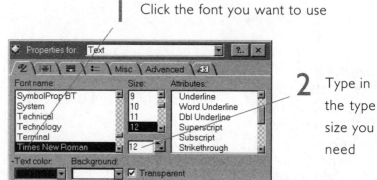

2 Type in the type size you need

The changes you make are automatically applied to the selected text.

Applying a new font or type size (2)

Select the text you want to amend and do either of the following:

HANDY TIP

You can use keyboard shortcuts here. Press F3 to apply the next font, F4 the next type size. (Pressing Shift with the function key reverses the direction.)

Click here repeatedly to step up alphabetically through the fonts on your system, one by one

Click here repeatedly to step up through type sizes in increments of 2 (e.g. from 6 to 8 to 10...)

Changing text colour

You can change the colour of text:

- from within the Text Properties Infobox

- by using the Status bar

Using the Infobox

First, select the text you want to alter. Pull down the Text menu and click Text Properties. Now do the following:

Click here

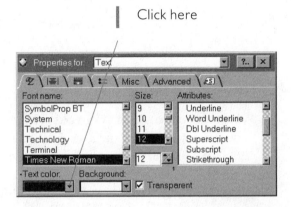

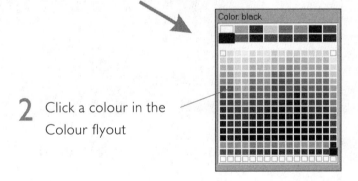

2 Click a colour in the Colour flyout

Using the Status bar

Select the text you want to alter. Carry out the action indicated below to launch the Colour flyout. Then follow step 2 above.

Click here

Changing font attributes

In WordPro, the principal typeface attributes you can apply are:

You can also use keyboard shortcuts: Ctrl+B to embolden selected text; Ctrl+I to italicise it; Ctrl+U to underline it; Ctrl+W to word-underline it; Ctrl+N to remove all attributes.

- Bold (**bold**) and Italic (*italic*)

- Underline (<u>underline</u>) and Word Underline (<u>word</u> <u>underline</u>)

- Strikethrough (~~strikethrough~~); Small Caps (SMALL CAPS); Superscript (superscript) and Subscript (subscript)

- Upper Case (UPPER CASE) and Lower Case (lower case)

You can use the Text Properties Infobox or a specific 'Cycle' SmartIcon to change font attributes.

Amending font attributes (1)

First, select the relevant text. Pull down the Text menu and click Text Properties. Now do the following:

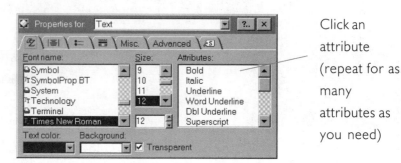

Click an attribute (repeat for as many attributes as you need)

Amending font attributes (2)

First, select the relevant text. Then do the following:

Click here repeatedly to step up through the attributes, one by one

Indenting paragraphs - an overview

Indents are a crucial component of document layout. For instance, in most document types indenting the first line of paragraphs (i.e. moving it inwards away from the left page margin) makes the text much more legible.

You can achieve a similar effect by using tabs. However, indents are easier to apply (and amend subsequently).

Other document types – e.g. bibliographies – can use the following:

- negative indents (where the direction of indent is towards and beyond the left margin)

- hanging indents (where the first line is unaltered, while subsequent lines are indented)

- full indents (where the entire paragraph is indented away from the left and/or right margins)

Don't confuse indents with page margins. Margins are the gap between the edge of the page and the text area; indents define the distance between the margins and text.

Some of the potential indent combinations are shown in the (generic) illustration below:

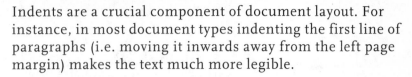

This paragraph has a full left and right indent. It's best, however, not to overdo the extent of the indent: 0.35 inches is often more than adequate.

    This paragraph has a first-line indent. This type of indent is suitable for most document types. It's best, however, not to overdo the extent of the indent: 0.35 inches is often more than adequate.

This paragraph has a negative left indent. It's best, however, not to overdo the extent of the indent: 0.35 inches is often more than adequate.

This paragraph has a hanging indent. It's best, however, not to overdo the extent of the indent: 0.35 inches is often more than adequate.

left and right indent

first-line indent

negative left indent

hanging indent

Left margin (inserted for illustration purposes)

Right margin (inserted for illustration purposes)

Indenting paragraphs

Paragraphs can be indented from within the Text Properties Infobox, or by using a 'Cycle' SmartIcon.

HANDY TIP

The Infobox indent buttons are:

 Left Indent

 First Line Indent

 Hanging Indent

 Full Indent

Indenting text (1)

First, select the paragraph you want to indent. Pull down the Text menu and click Text Properties. Now do the following:

Click the Alignment tab

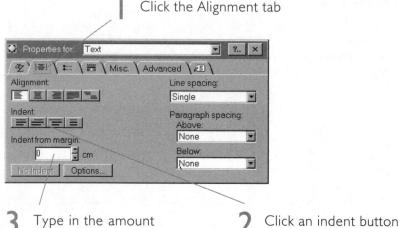

HANDY TIP

Re step 3 - type in minus values for negative indents.

3 Type in the amount of indent

2 Click an indent button

Indenting text (2)

First, select the relevant text. Then do the following:

Click here repeatedly to step up through indent types, one by one

HANDY TIP

You can use a keyboard shortcut here. Press F7 to increment Left Indent (or Shift+F7 to decrement it).

Note, however, that the Indent Cycle SmartIcon only applies Left Indent.

Aligning paragraphs

The following are the principal types of alignment:

Left
Text is flush with the left page margin.

Center
Text is aligned equidistantly between the left and right page margins.

Right
Text is flush with the right page margin.

Justified
Text is flush with the left *and* right page margins

The Infobox alignment buttons are:

 Left

 Center

 Right

 Justified

You can align text from within the Text Properties Infobox, or by using a 'Cycle' SmartIcon.

Aligning text (1)
Select the paragraph(s) you want to indent. Pull down the Text menu and click Text Properties. Now do the following:

Click the Alignment tab

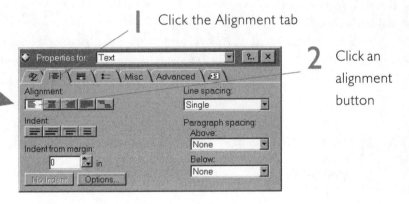

2 Click an alignment button

You can use a keyboard shortcut here. Press F6 to step through alignment options (or Shift+F6 to reverse the direction).

Aligning text (2)
Select the relevant paragraph(s). Then do the following:

Click here repeatedly to step up through alignment types

Specifying paragraph spacing

You can customise the vertical space before and/or after specific text paragraphs. This is a useful device for increasing text legibility.

You can only adjust paragraph spacing from within the Text Properties Infobox.

By default, SmartSuite defines paragraph spacing in terms of preset line measurements (e.g. 1.5 or 2 lines). However, if none of these are suitable you can specify your own number of lines, or enter measurements in different units (picas, inches, centimetres or points).

Applying paragraph spacing (1)

First, select the paragraph(s) whose spacing you want to adjust. Pull down the Text menu and click Text Properties. Then carry out steps 1-2 below.

As a general rule, set low paragraph spacing settings: a little goes a long way.

Points are a unit in typography: 72 points are roughly equivalent to one inch. Picas are an alternative measure in typography (1 pica is almost equivalent to one-sixth of an inch) and are often used to define line length.

Re step 2 - click Multiple to set your own line multiple (and then follow steps 3-4); or click Custom to set your own spacing using a different unit (and then follow steps 5-7).

1 Click the Alignment tab

2 Click either location; select a preset spacing. Alternatively, click Multiple or Custom (see the 'Handy Tip').

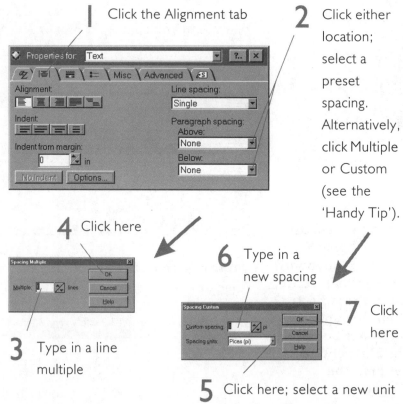

4 Click here

6 Type in a new spacing

7 Click here

3 Type in a line multiple

5 Click here; select a new unit

Line spacing - an overview

It's often necessary to amend line spacing. This is the vertical distance between individual lines of text, or more accurately between the baseline (the imaginary line on which text appears to sit) of one line and the baseline of the previous.

Line spacing is also known as leading (pronounced 'ledding').

WordPro lets you apply preset line spacings – Single, ½, 1½ and Double.

Alternatively, you can:

•   specify your own line multiples (e.g. 4 – four lines)

•   specify a number followed by a measurement in inches, centimetres, picas or points (e.g. 2 points, 0.167 picas)

•   specify a leading addition (where the spacing you choose is *added to* the type size). In other words, if you specify a leading adjustment of 4 points on text which is set at 13 points, the resultant spacing is 17 points.

This paragraph is in single line spacing. Newspapers frequently use this.

This paragraph is in 1½ line spacing. Probably no one uses this, but it serves as a useful illustration.

This paragraph is in double line spacing; writers use this when preparing manuscripts

Single line spacing

1.5 line spacing

Double line spacing

Adjusting line spacing

First, select the relevant paragraph(s). Then pull down the Text menu and click Text Properties. Carry out steps 1-2:

HANDY TIP

If you've just created a new document, you can set the line spacing before you begin to enter text. Simply leave the insertion point at the start of the document, and then follow the procedures outlined here.

REMEMBER

Re step 2 - click Multiple to set your own line multiple (and then follow steps 3-4). Or click Custom to set your own spacing using a different unit (and then follow steps 5-7). Alternatively, click Leading to set a leading addition (and then follow steps 8-10).

1 Click the Alignment tab

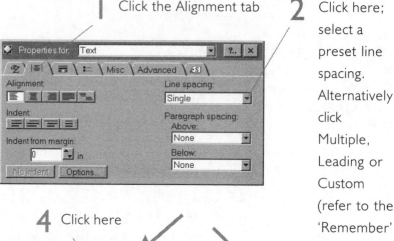

2 Click here; select a preset line spacing. Alternatively, click Multiple, Leading or Custom (refer to the 'Remember' tip).

4 Click here

3 Type in a line multiple

6 Type in a new spacing

7 Click here

5 Click here; select a new unit

9 Type in a leading addition

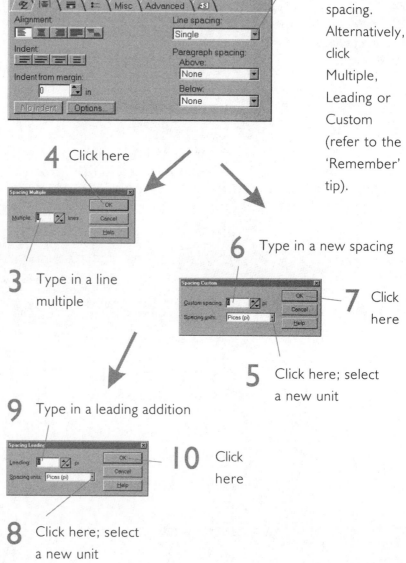

10 Click here

8 Click here; select a new unit

Paragraph borders

By default, WordPro does not border paragraph text. However, you can apply a wide selection of borders if you want. You can specify:

- the border type and thickness

- how many sides the border should have

- the border colour

- whether the bordered text should have a drop shadow

- the distance between the border and the enclosed text

Applying a border

First, select the paragraph(s) you want to border. Then pull down the Text menu and click Text Properties. Follow steps 1-6, as appropriate (if you carry out step 6, also follow 7).

HANDY TIP

Re step 2 - click the final icon on the right if you want to border all four sides of the selected paragraph(s) and apply a drop shadow.

HANDY TIP

If you want the border to stretch from the left to right margins, click in the Line length field; select To margins.

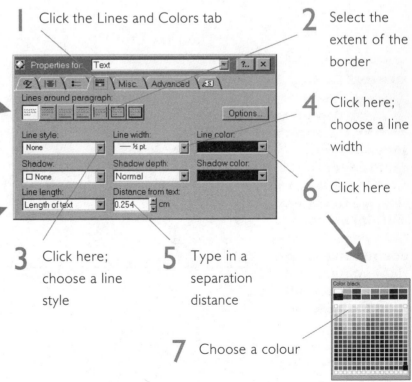

1 Click the Lines and Colors tab

2 Select the extent of the border

4 Click here; choose a line width

6 Click here

3 Click here; choose a line style

5 Type in a separation distance

7 Choose a colour

Working with tabs

Tabs are a means of indenting the first line of text paragraphs (you can also use indents for this purpose, although tabs are probably more convenient for single paragraphs).

Never use the Space bar to indent paragraphs: spaces vary in size according to the typeface and type size applied to specific paragraphs.

When you press the Tab key while the text insertion point is at the start of a paragraph, the text in the first line jumps to the next tab stop. This is a useful way to increase the legibility of your text. WordPro lets you set tab stops with great precision.

By default, tab stops are inserted automatically every quarter of an inch. If you want, however, you can enter new or revised tab stop positions individually.

Setting tab stops

First, select the paragraph(s) in which you need to set tab stops. Pull down the Text menu and click Text Properties. Follow steps 1-3 below:

Re step 2 - if you don't want to enter a series of tabs, choose From left edge (to enter a tab relative to the left margin) or From right edge (to enter one relative to the right margin). Alternatively, click Remove local tabs to remove previously assigned tab settings.

I Click the Misc tab

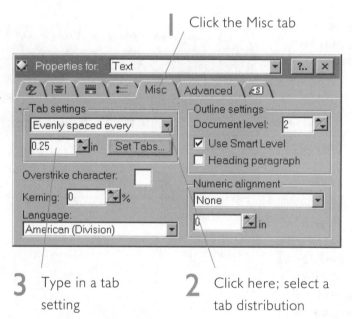

3 Type in a tab setting

2 Click here; select a tab distribution

Searching for text

WordPro lets you search for specific text within the active document.

You can also search for special characters. For example, you can look for paragraph marks, tabs, wildcards and ^ characters.

You can also:

- limit the search to words which match the case of the text you specify (e.g. if you search for 'Arm', SmartSuite will not flag 'arm' or 'ARM')

- limit the search to whole words (e.g. if you search for 'eat', SmartSuite will not flag 'beat' or 'meat')

Initiating a text search

Pull down the Edit menu and click Find and Replace Text. Now carry out the following steps, as appropriate:

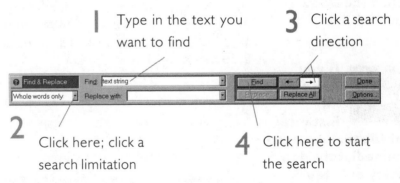

| Type in the text you want to find

3 Click a search direction

2 Click here; click a search limitation

4 Click here to start the search

Entering codes

When you complete step 1, you can enter the following:

^t	Tab
^r	Paragraph mark
^ ^	^
^?	any one character
^*	any number of characters

When you've finished using the Find & Replace bar, click the Done button.

Re step 3 - click the left-pointing arrow to search backwards, or the right-pointing arrow to search towards the end of the document.

The SmartSuite wildcards, '?' and '*', are very useful. For instance, searching for 'me?t' would find 'meet' or 'meat'. Searching for 'le*' would find 'lend', 'leap', 'lexicography' etc.

Replacing text

When you've searched for and located text in the active document, you can have WordPro replace it automatically with the text of your choice.

You can customise find-and-replace operations with the same parameters as a simple find operation. For example, you can make them case-specific, or only replace whole words. You can also incorporate a variety of codes (for how to do this, see the 'Searching for text' topic earlier in this section). For instance, you could have WordPro locate instances of two paragraph marks and replace them with a single mark.

There is, however, one way in which find-and-replace operations differ from find operations: wildcards can't be incorporated in replacement text.

When you've finished using the Find & Replace bar, click the Done button.

Initiating a find-and-replace operation

First pull down the Edit menu and click Find & Replace Text. Now follow steps 1 and 2 below. Carry out steps 3 and 4, as appropriate. Finally, follow step 5 to perform all valid find-and-replace operations automatically (or see the associated tip):

If you don't want all instances of the text replaced immediately, don't carry out step 5. Instead, click the Find button after step 4. When the first match has been found, click Replace. Repeat this as often as necessary.

1 Type in the text you want to find

2 Type in the replacement text

3 Click a search direction

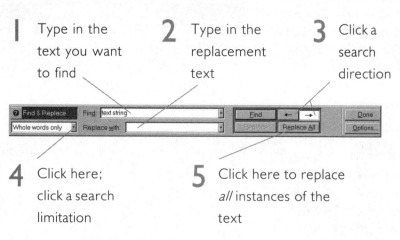

4 Click here; click a search limitation

5 Click here to replace *all* instances of the text

Working with headers

You can have WordPro display and print text at the top of each page within a document; the area of the page where repeated text appears is called the 'header'. In the same way, you can have text printed at the base of each page; in this case, the relevant page area is called the 'footer'. Headers and footers are printed within the top and bottom page margins, respectively.

Headers and footers are commonly used to display document titles, origination details and page numbers.

Inserting a header

In Layout view (headers and footers are not visible in Draft view), move to the top of the first page, then click in the Header area. Now do the following:

To edit an existing header, simply follow the procedure outlined here; in step 1, amend the current header text as necessary.

Re step 1 - to have WordPro insert a special code which automatically inserts the page number in the header, pull down the Text menu and click Insert Page Number. When the Insert Page Number dialog appears, click OK.

Header text (and numbers) can be formatted in the normal way. For instance, you can apply a new font and/or type size.

Type in the Header text

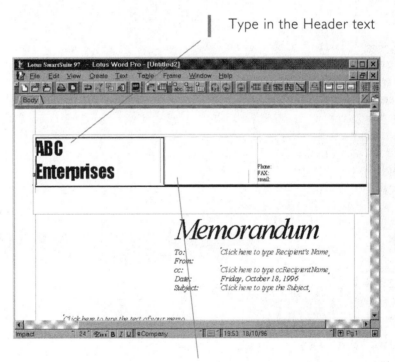

The Header area

Working with footers

You can have WordPro automatically display and print text at the bottom of each page within a document. The area of the page where this repeated text appears is called the 'footer'.

Footers are often used to display an abbreviated version of the document's title and/or the page number.

Inserting a footer

In Layout view, move to the bottom of the first page then click in the Footer area. Do the following:

To edit an existing footer, simply follow the procedure outlined here; in step 1, amend the current footer text as necessary.

Re step 1 - to have WordPro insert a special code which automatically inserts the page number in the footer, pull down the Text menu and click Insert Page Number. When the Insert Page Number dialog appears, click OK.

Footer text (and numbers) can be formatted in the normal way. For instance, you can apply a new font and/or type size.

Type in the Footer text

The Footer area

Undo

To set the number of Undo levels, pull down the File menu and click User Setup, WordPro Preferences. In the WordPro Preferences dialog, click the General tab. In the Undo levels field, type in the number. Click OK.

WordPro lets you reverse – 'undo' – most editing operations.

You can undo the last editing action in the following ways:

- via the keyboard

- from within the Edit menu

- by using a SmartIcon

Using the keyboard
Simply press Ctrl+Z to undo an action.

Using the Edit menu
Pull down the Edit menu. To undo an action, do the following:

The precise text of the menu entry depends on the action being undone.

Click here

Using the Undo SmartIcon
To undo an operation, click the following SmartIcon in the overhead SmartIcon bar:

Text styles - an overview

Styles are named collections of associated formatting commands. WordPro makes extensive use of styles in all areas, but particularly when it comes to text formatting.

The advantage of using styles is that you can apply more than one formatting enhancement to selected text in one go. Once a style is in place, you can easily change one or more elements of it and have WordPro apply the amendments automatically throughout the whole of the active document. This results in an enormous saving in time and effort.

New (blank) documents you create in WordPro contain a variety of pre-defined styles. These include:

- *Body Single* – used for body text

- *Default Text* – ditto

- *Bullet 1* and *Bullet 2* – create bulleted lists

- *Heading 1* – used for headings

- *Heading 2* – ditto (but smaller)

- *Heading 3* – ditto (even smaller)

- *Title* – a rather ornate heading

- *Number List* – creates automatically numbered lists

- *First Line Indent* – automatically applies a preset paragraph indent

Other templates/SmartMasters have many more preset styles. (Some are context-dependent, e.g. *Default Page* only applies to page settings, not specific text.)

You can easily create (and apply) your own styles.

Creating a text style

Creating a style is a simple, two-stage process:

1. Apply the appropriate formatting enhancements to selected text;

2. Tell WordPro to save this formatting as a style.

First, carry out step 1 above. Then pull down the Text menu and click Text Properties. Now do the following:

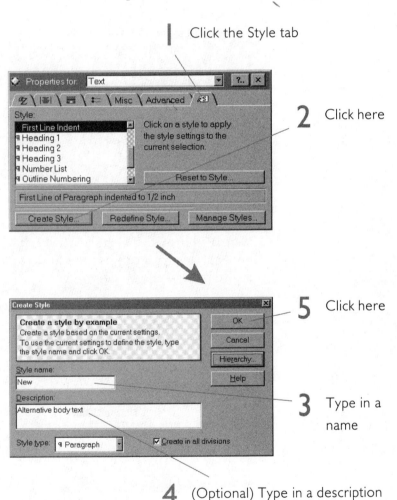

Click the Style tab

2 Click here

5 Click here

3 Type in a name

4 (Optional) Type in a description

HANDY TIP

If you want to create a character (as opposed to a paragraph) style, click the arrow to the right of the Style Type field; select Character in the drop-down list.

See 'Applying a text style' on the following page for how to use your new style.

Applying a text style

WordPro makes applying styles easy.

First, select the text you want to apply the style to. Or, if you only want to apply it to a single paragraph, place the insertion point inside it. Pull down the Text menu and click Text Properties. Now do the following:

Click the Style tab

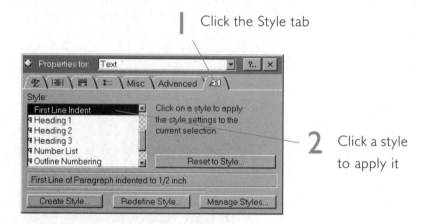

2 Click a style to apply it

Shortcut for applying styles

WordPro provides a shortcut which makes it even easier to apply styles: you can use the Style button on the Status bar at the base of the screen.

Select the text you want to apply the style to. Then do the following:

2 Click a style

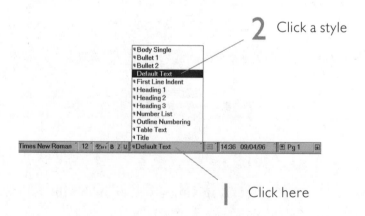

Click here

Amending a text style

The easiest way to modify an existing style is to:

1. Use the Text Properties Infobox to apply the appropriate formatting enhancements to text (see earlier topics for information on how to do this) and then select it.

2. Tell WordPro to redefine the associated style based on your amendments.

First, carry out step 1 above. Then do the following:

When you redefine a style, all other instances of the style in the open document are automatically updated accordingly.

Click the Style tab

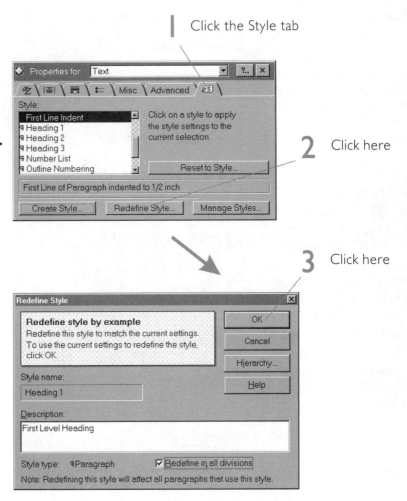

2 Click here

3 Click here

Style management

Good housekeeping sometimes makes it necessary to remove unwanted styles from the active document. WordPro lets you do this very easily.

Deleting styles

Pull down the Text menu and click Text Properties. Now do the following:

 You can delete more than one style at a time. Simply repeat step 3 as often as required, then follow steps 4-6 as normal.

Click the Style tab

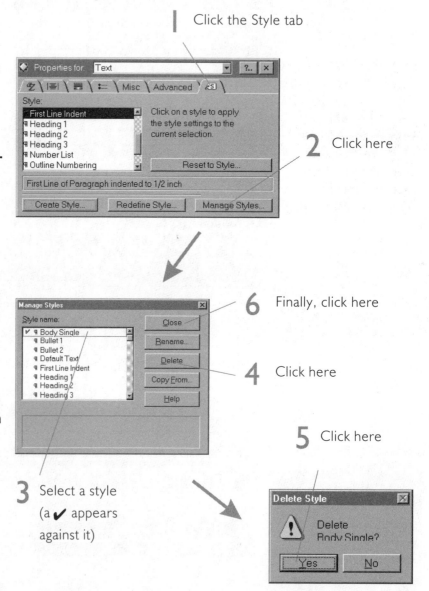

2 Click here

 You can also use this dialog to rename a specified style. Simply click it then click the Rename button. In the To field in the Rename Style dialog, type in a new name. Then click OK. Finally, follow step 6.

6 Finally, click here

4 Click here

5 Click here

3 Select a style (a ✔ appears against it)

Spell-checking text

SmartSuite makes use of two separate dictionaries. One - LTSUSER1.UDC - can be thought of as yours. When you follow step 4, the flagged word is stored in this and recognised in future checking sessions.

If the flagged word isn't correct and WordPro's suggestions are also wrong, type in the correct version in the Replace with field. Then carry out step 2 or 3.

Click the Done button when you're ready to close the Spell Check bar.

To check all the text within the active document in one go, pull down the Edit menu and click Check Spelling. WordPro launches its Spell Check bar, highlights all words it doesn't recognise within the current document and takes you to the first (flagged with a different colour). Usually, it provides alternative suggestions; if one of these is correct, you can opt to have it replace the flagged word. You can do this singly (i.e. just this instance is replaced) or globally (where all future instances – within the current checking session – are replaced).

Alternatively, you can have SmartSuite:

- ignore *this* instance of the flagged word and resume checking

- ignore *all* future instances of the word and resume checking

- add the word to your personal dictionary and resume checking

Carry out step 1 below (if WordPro has produced a viable suggestion). Then follow step 2 or 3, *or* any one of steps 4, 5 and 6.

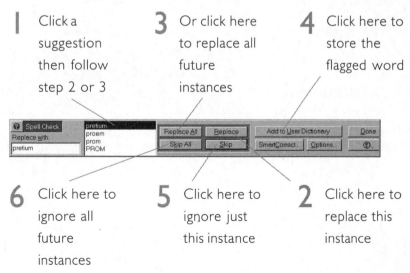

1 Click a suggestion then follow step 2 or 3

3 Or click here to replace all future instances

4 Click here to store the flagged word

6 Click here to ignore all future instances

5 Click here to ignore just this instance

2 Click here to replace this instance

Searching for synonyms

WordPro lets you search for synonyms while you're editing the active document. You do this by calling up the resident Thesaurus. The Thesaurus categorises words into meanings, and each meaning is allocated various synonyms from which you can choose.

The Thesaurus works in two ways. You can flag a word in the document and have it propose synonyms (the more usual method). Alternatively, you can enter words *directly* into the Thesaurus and request suggestions.

Using the Thesaurus

First, select the word for which you require a synonym (or simply position the insertion point within it). Pull down the Edit menu and click Check Thesaurus. Now do the following:

HANDY TIP

To look up a word which isn't in the current document, type it into the Word to look up or to be replaced field. Then click the Lookup button. Now carry out steps 1-3, as appropriate.

The selected word appears here

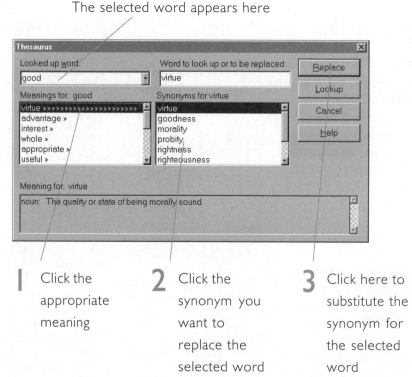

Thesaurus
Looked up word:
good
Meanings for: good
virtue »»»»»»»»»»»»»»»»»»»
advantage »
interest »
whole »
appropriate »
useful »

Word to look up or to be replaced:
virtue

Synonyms for virtue
virtue
goodness
morality
probity
rightness
righteousness

Replace
Lookup
Cancel
Help

Meaning for: virtue

noun: The quality or state of being morally sound

1 Click the appropriate meaning

2 Click the synonym you want to replace the selected word

3 Click here to substitute the synonym for the selected word

Working with pictures - an overview

The WordPro module lets you add colour or greyscale pictures to the active document. Pictures – also called graphics – include:

- drawings produced in other programs

- clip art

- scanned photographs

Use pictures – whatever their source – to add much needed visual impact to documents. But use them judiciously: too much colour can be off-putting, and ultimately self-defeating.

Pictures are stored in various third-party formats. These formats are organised into two basic types:

Bitmap images

Bitmaps consist of pixels (dots) arranged in such a way that they form a graphic image. Because of the very nature of bitmaps, the question of 'resolution' – the sharpness of an image expressed in dpi (dots per inch) – is very important. Bitmaps look best if they're displayed at their native resolution. WordPro can manipulate a wide variety of third-party bitmap graphics formats. These include PCX, TIF and GIF.

Vector images

You can also insert vector graphics files into WordPro documents. Vector images (e.g. CGM) consist of and are defined by algebraic equations. Less complex than bitmaps, they contain less detail. Vector files can also include bitmap information.

Irrespective of the format type, SmartSuite can incorporate pictures with the help of special 'filters'. These are special mini-programs whose job it is to translate third-party formats into a form which SmartSuite can use.

Brief notes on picture formats

Graphics formats SmartSuite will accept include the following (the column on the left shows the relevant file suffix):

CGM Computer Graphics Metafile. A vector format frequently used in the past, especially as a medium for clip-art transmission. Less often used nowadays.

EPS Encapsulated PostScript. Perhaps the most widely used PostScript format. PostScript combines vector *and* bitmap data very successfully. Incorporates a low-resolution bitmap 'header' for preview purposes.

GIF Graphics Interchange Format. Developed for the on-line transmission of graphics data across the CompuServe network. Just about any Windows program – and a lot more besides – will read GIF. Disadvantage: it can't handle more than 256 colours. Compression is supported.

PCD (Kodak) PhotoCD. Used primarily to store photographs on CD.

PCX An old standby. Originated with PC Paintbrush, a paint program. Used for years to transfer graphics data between Windows applications.

CDR Files produced by version 3 of the popular drawing package CorelDRAW! from Corel Corporation. (Later versions of CorelDRAW! will happily export files to version 3's format).

TIF TIFF, or Tagged Image File Format. If anything, even more widely used than PCX, across a whole range of platforms and applications.

Inserting pictures

First, position the insertion point at the location within the active document where you want to insert the picture. Pull down the File menu and do the following:

WordPro creates special 'snapshot' files for inserted pictures. These enable WordPro to display pictures rapidly in open documents.

Click here

Now carry out the following steps:

2 Click here. In the drop-down list, click the drive/folder that hosts the file

3 Click the file

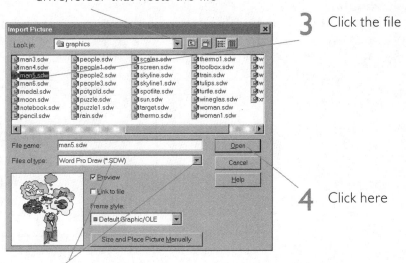

Make sure Preview is selected for an indication of what a picture will look like when inserted.

4 Click here

Make sure the relevant file type is shown. If it isn't, click the arrow and select it from the drop-down list

Manipulating pictures - an overview

Once you've inserted pictures into a WordPro document, you can amend them in a variety of ways. You can:

- rescale them

- apply a border

- move them

Selecting an image

To carry out any of these operations, you have to select the relevant picture first. To do this, simply position the mouse pointer over the image and left-click once. SmartSuite surrounds the image with eight handles (and also with a frame – see the tip on the left). Handles are positioned at the four corners, and midway on each side. The illustration below demonstrates these (two of the handles are magnified for convenience):

REMEMBER

By default, WordPro surrounds inserted graphics with a frame. Frames make pictures easier to manipulate; they even have their own Frame Properties Infobox.

Handles

SmartSuite is great!

Rescaling pictures

There are two ways in which you can rescale pictures:

- proportionately, where the height/width ratio remains constant

- disproportionately, where the height/width ratio is disrupted (this is sometimes called 'warping' or 'skewing')

 By default, WordPro rescales images proportionately. To warp a picture, do the following before you rescale it. With the image selected, click Frame Properties in the Frame menu. In the Frame Properties Infobox (see the excerpt below), click the Misc tab.

To rescale a picture, first select it. Then move the mouse pointer over:

- one of the corner handles, if you want to rescale the image in any direction;

or

- one of the handles in the middle of the sides, if you want to rescale it laterally

In either eventuality, the mouse pointer changes to a double-headed arrow. Click and hold down the left mouse button. Drag outwards to increase the image size or inwards to decrease it. Release the mouse button to confirm the change.

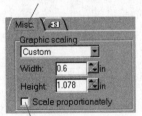

Now deselect Scale proportionately.

Another WordPro image, this time skewed from the right inwards

Bordering pictures

By default, WordPro applies an even border to inserted pictures (within the holding frame). However, you can change this, if you want. You can specify:

- the border type and thickness

- whether the bordered image should have a drop shadow

- how many sides the border should have

- the border colour

Applying a border

HANDY TIP

Re step 2 - click the middle icon if you want to border all 4 sides of the selected paragraph(s) and apply a drop shadow.

Select the image whose border you want to amend. Pull down the Frame menu and click Frame Properties. Follow steps 1-6, as needed (if you carry out step 6, also follow 7).

1 Click the Lines tab

2 Select the extent of the border

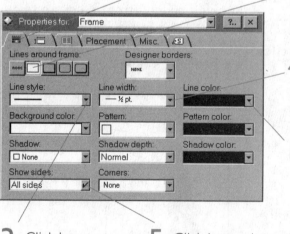

4 Click here; choose a line width

6 Click here

3 Click here; choose a style

5 Click here; choose which sides display

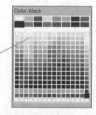

7 Choose a colour

Moving pictures

You can easily move pictures from one location on the page to another.

First, click the image to select it. Move the mouse pointer over it; it changes to an open hand. Left-click once and hold down the button. Drag the picture to its new location.

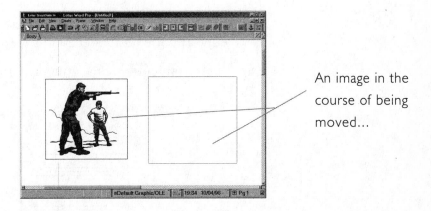

An image in the course of being moved...

Release the mouse button to confirm the move.

Problems with Move operations?

If you find that dragging pictures has no effect, select the image. Pull down the Frame menu and click Frame Properties. Carry out the following steps:

Click the Placement tab

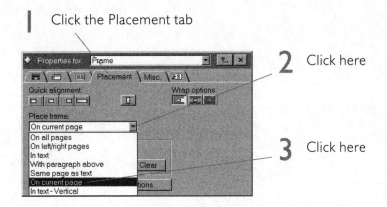

2 Click here

3 Click here

Now carry out the move again.

Page setup - an overview

You can control the following aspects of page layout in the WordPro module:

- the top, bottom, left and/or right page margins

- the distance above the header (between the top page edge and the top edge of the header)

- the distance below the footer (between the bottom page edge and the bottom edge of the footer)

The illustration below shows the principal components:

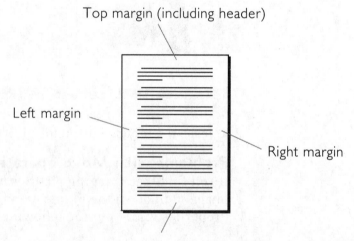

Top margin (including header)

Left margin

Right margin

Bottom margin (including footer)

You can also specify:

- the overall page size (inclusive of margins and headers/footers)

- the page orientation ('landscape' or 'portrait')

If none of the supplied page sizes is suitable, you can even customise your own.

Specifying margins

All documents have margins because they need a certain amount of 'white space' (the unprinted portion of the page) to balance the areas which contain text and graphics. Margins make documents more visually effective.

REMEMBER

Margin settings are the framework on which indents and tabs are based.

Customising document margins

Pull down the File menu and click Document Properties, Page. Now do the following:

Click here

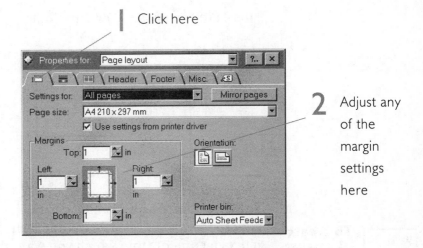

2 Adjust any of the margin settings here

Customising header/footer margins

To adjust header margins, pull down the File menu and click Document Properties, Page. Now do the following:

HANDY TIP

To amend footer margins, launch the Frame Properties Infobox. Click the Footer tab. Now adjust the Below footer field.

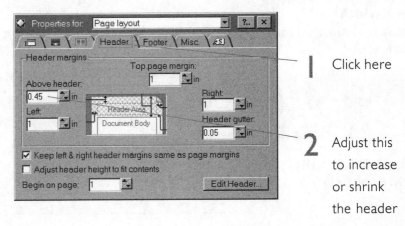

Click here

2 Adjust this to increase or shrink the header

Specifying the page size

WordPro comes with several preset page sizes. These are suitable for most purposes. However, if you need to you can also set up your own page definition.

There are two aspects to every page size:

- a vertical measurement

- a horizontal measurement

There are two possible orientations:

Portrait   Landscape

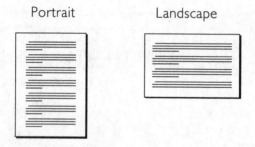

Setting the page size

To create your own page size, click Custom in step 2. Then type in height and width measurements (see below):

First, position the insertion point at the location within the active document from which you want the new page size to apply. Then pull down the File menu and click Document Properties, Page. Now do the following:

Click here

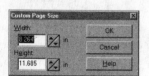

Click OK. Finally, carry out step 3.

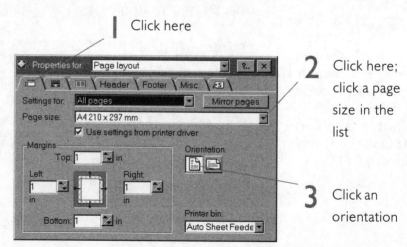

2 Click here; click a page size in the list

3 Click an orientation

Print setup

Most WordPro documents need to be printed eventually. Before you can begin printing, however, you need to ensure that:

- the correct printer is selected (if you have more than one installed)

- the correct printer settings are in force

SmartSuite calls these collectively 'Print Setup'.

Irrespective of the printer selected, the settings (step 2 below) vary in accordance with the job in hand. For example, most printer drivers (the software that 'drives' the printer) allow you to specify whether or not you want pictures printed. Additionally, they often allow you to specify the resolution or print quality of the output.

Selecting the printer and/or settings

Just before you're ready to print a document, pull down the File menu and click Document Properties, Print Setup. Now do the following:

1 Click here; select the printer you want from the list

3 Click here

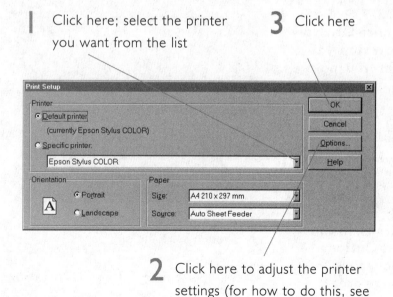

2 Click here to adjust the printer settings (for how to do this, see your printer's manual)

Customised printing

Once the active document is how you want it (and you've customised the print setup appropriately), the next stage is to print it out. WordPro makes this process easy and lets you set a variety of options before you do so. These include:

- the number of copies you want printed

Re step 2 – this prints a *single* page range. **To print multiple ranges, click the Select Pages button.**

- whether you want the copies 'collated' (one full copy printed at a time). For instance, if you're printing three copies of a 40-page document, SmartSuite prints pages 1-40 of the first document, followed by pages 1-40 of the second and pages 1-40 of the third.

- only printing odd or even pages

Starting to print

Pull down the File menu and click Print. Now carry out steps 1-4 below, as appropriate.

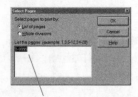

Type in page ranges (e.g. 3-7, 9, 6-15) and click OK. Now follow step 4 to begin printing.

4 Click here to initiate printing

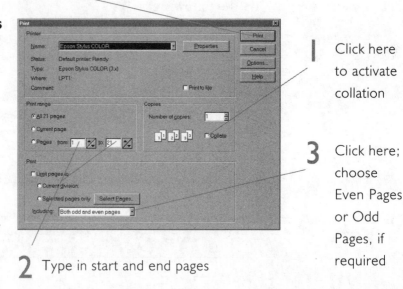

1 Click here to activate collation

3 Click here; choose Even Pages or Odd Pages, if required

To print the last page first, click Options. In the Print Options dialog, click In reverse order.

2 Type in start and end pages

After step 4, SmartSuite starts printing the active document.

1-2-3

This chapter gives you the fundamentals of using 1-2-3. You'll learn how to work with data and formulas, and how to move around through worksheets. You'll also learn how to make your data more visually effective with the use of charts. Finally, you'll customise page layout/printing.

Covers

The 1-2-3 screen

Below is a detailed illustration of the 1-2-3 screen.

Title bar   Menu bar   Contents box

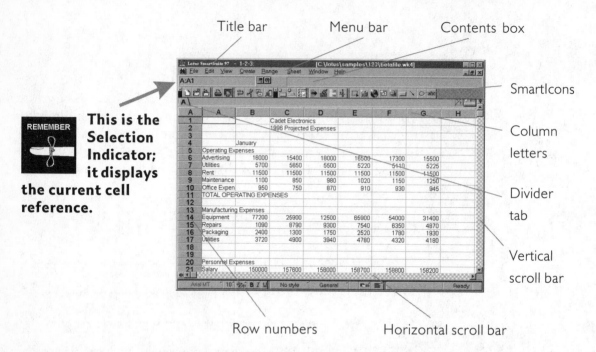

SmartIcons

REMEMBER

This is the Selection Indicator; it displays the current cell reference.

Column letters

Divider tab

Vertical scroll bar

Row numbers   Horizontal scroll bar

Some of these screen components can be hidden.

Specifying which screen components display

Pull down the View menu and click Set View Preferences. Then do the following:

Click here

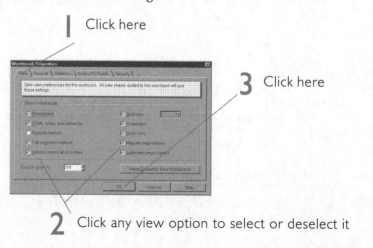

3 Click here

2 Click any view option to select or deselect it

Entering data (1)

When you start 1-2-3, you can use the Welcome screen to produce a new blank worksheet (see Section 1 for how to do this). The result will look something like this:

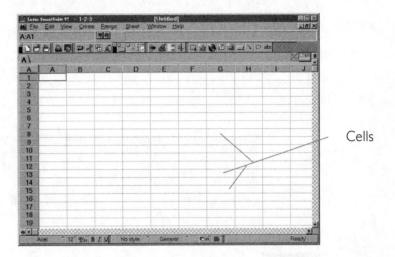

Cells

This means that you can start entering data immediately.

In 1-2-3, you can enter the following basic data types:

- values (i.e. numbers)

- text (e.g. headings and explanatory material)

- functions (e.g. Sine or Cosine)

- formulas (combinations of values, text and functions)

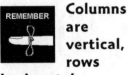

REMEMBER

Columns are vertical, rows horizontal.

You enter data into 'cells'. Cells are formed where rows and columns intersect. In the figure above, cells G8, G13 and G15 are flagged for illustration purposes.

Collections of rows/columns and cells are known in 1-2-3 as worksheets. Worksheets are organised into files known as workbooks. Each workbook can have numerous worksheets, if required.

Entering data (2)

Although you can enter data *directly* into a cell (by simply clicking in it and typing it in), there's another method you can use which is often easier. 1-2-3 provides a special screen component known as the Contents box.

The illustration below shows a section of the worksheet created with the Create an Invoice SmartMaster. Cell C7 is currently flagged in the Selection Indicator.

Selection Indicator

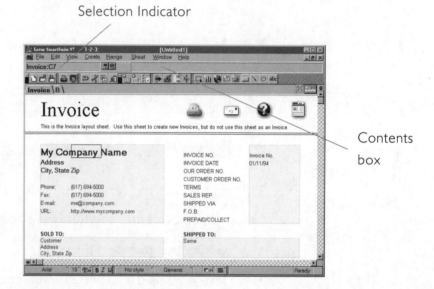

Contents box

Entering data via the Contents box

Click the cell you want to insert data into. Then click the Contents box. Type in the data. Then follow step 1 below. If you decide not to proceed with the operation, follow step 2 instead:

You can use a keyboard route to confirm operations in the Contents box: simply press Return.

1 Click here

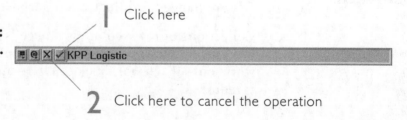

2 Click here to cancel the operation

Modifying existing data

You can amend the contents of a cell in two ways:

- via the Contents box

- from within the cell

When you use either of these methods, 1-2-3 enters a special state known as Edit Mode.

Amending existing data using the Contents box

Click the cell whose contents you want to change. Then click in the Contents box. Make the appropriate revisions and/or additions. Then press Return. 1-2-3 updates the relevant cell.

Amending existing data internally

Click the cell whose contents you want to change. Press F2. Make the appropriate revisions and/or additions *within the cell*. Then press Return.

The illustration below shows a further section of the worksheet based on the Create an Invoice SmartMaster.

Cell H23, in Edit Mode

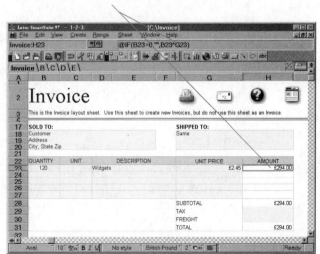

Working with cell ranges

When you're working with more than one cell, it's often convenient and useful to organise them in 'ranges'.

A range is a rectangular arrangement of cells. In the illustration below, cells C19, C20, D19, D20, E19, E20, F19, F20, G19, G20, H19, H20, I19 and I20 have been selected.

A selected cell range

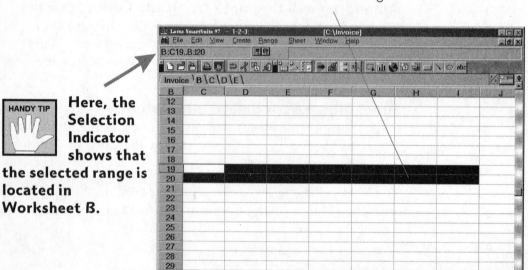

HANDY TIP

Here, the Selection Indicator shows that the selected range is located in Worksheet B.

The above description is very cumbersome. It's much more useful to use a form of shorthand. 1-2-3 (using the start and end cells as reference points) refers to these cells as:

C19..I20

This can be extended even more – see the Selection Indicator above – in that cell addresses can also refer to the host worksheet. In this case, our address becomes:

B:C19..B:I20

denoting that the start and end cells are in Worksheet B.

Moving around in worksheets (1)

HANDY TIP

When you drag the vertical or horizontal scroll box, 1-2-3 displays a box indicating which row or column you're up to:

Row: 12

1-2-3 worksheets are huge. Moving to cells which happen currently to be visible is easy: you simply click in the relevant cell. However, 1-2-3 provides several techniques you can use to jump to less accessible areas.

Using the scroll bars

Use any of the following methods:

1. To scroll quickly to another section of the active worksheet, drag the scroll box along the scroll bar until you reach it.

2. To jump to the left or right, click to the left or right of the scroll box in the horizontal scroll bar.

3. To jump up or down, click above or below the scroll box in the vertical scroll bar.

HANDY TIP

You can use your mouse to move to any other worksheet: simply click the appropriate divider tab (see the sample below):

Invoice \ B \ C \ D \ E \

4. To move up or down by one row, click the appropriate arrow in the vertical scroll bar.

5. To move left or right by one column, click the appropriate arrow in the horizontal scroll bar.

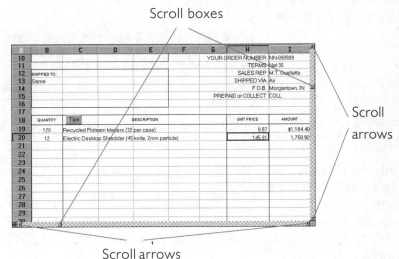

Scroll boxes

Scroll arrows

Scroll arrows

Moving around in worksheets (2)

In files that host more than one worksheet, press Ctrl+Page Up to jump to the next, or Ctrl+Page Down to move to the previous.

Using the keyboard

You can use the following techniques:

1. Use the cursor keys to move one cell left, right, up or down.

2. Press Ctrl+← to jump left by the number of columns visible, or Ctrl+→ to jump right by the same amount.

3. Press Home to jump to cell A1.

4. Press Page Up or Page Down to move up or down by one screen.

5. Press End+Home to move to the lower right-hand corner of the currently occupied cells.

Using the Go To dialog

1-2-3 provides a special dialog which you can use to specify precise cell destinations (particularly useful in very large worksheets).

You can use a keyboard shortcut to launch the Go To dialog: simply press F5.

Pull down the Edit menu and click Go To. Now do the following:

Re step 1 – a cell's 'reference' (or 'address') identifies it in relation to its position in a worksheet, e.g. ßll or H23. You can also type in cell ranges here.

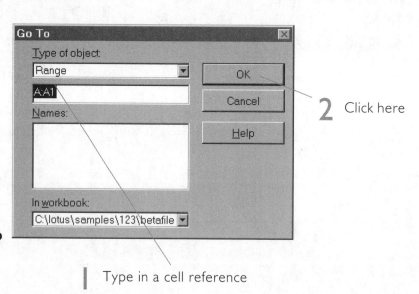

2 Click here

Type in a cell reference

Other operations on worksheets

It was said earlier that 1-2-3 files can contain numerous worksheets. You can easily:

- add new worksheets

- delete existing worksheets

- rename worksheets

HANDY TIP

To rename a worksheet, double-click its tab. Type in the new name and press Return.

Inserting a single worksheet

Right-click the tab that represents the sheet to the right of which you want the new worksheet inserted. In the menu that appears, click Create Sheet. In the Create Sheet dialog, click OK.

Inserting more than one worksheet

To add multiple worksheets, launch the Create Sheet dialog (see above). Then do the following:

HANDY TIP

If you want to specify the sheet placement, click an option here: *before* **you carry out step 2.**

Type in the no. of sheets

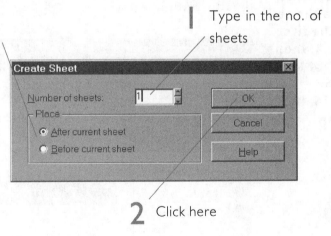

2 Click here

BEWARE

When you delete a worksheet, you automatically erase the worksheet contents, too.

Deleting a worksheet

Right-click the worksheet you want to remove. In the menu that launches, click Delete Sheet. Deletion is immediate: *1-2-3 does not launch a warning message first.*

If you delete a sheet in error, press Ctrl+Z *immediately* to reinstate it.

Selection techniques (1)

Before you can carry out any editing operations on cells in 1-2-3, you have to select them first. Selecting a single cell is very easy: you merely click in it. However, 1-2-3 provides a variety of selection techniques which you can use to select more than one cell.

With the exception of the first cell, a selected range is filled with black.

Selecting adjacent cell ranges

The easiest way to do this is to use the mouse. Click in the first cell in the range; hold down the left mouse button and drag over the remaining cells. Release the mouse button.

You can use the keyboard, too. Position the cell pointer over the first cell in the range. Hold down one Shift key as you use the cursor keys to extend the selection. Release the keys when the correct selection has been defined.

Selecting separate cell ranges

1-2-3 lets you select more than one range at a time. Look at the illustration below:

You can use another keyboard route. Place the cell pointer in the first cell. Press F4, then use the cursor keys to define the selection. Finally, press Return.

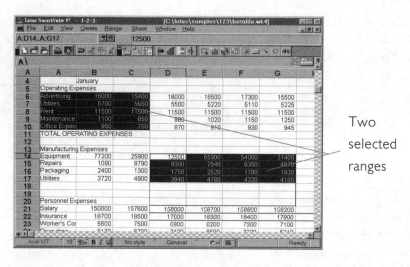

Two selected ranges

To select joint ranges, select the first in the normal way (note that you can't use the F4 method – see the tip – for this). Then hold down Ctrl as you select subsequent ranges.

Selection techniques (2)

Selecting a single row or column

To select every cell within a row or column automatically, click on the row or column heading.

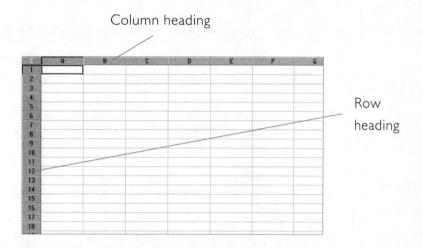

Column heading

Row heading

Selecting multiple rows or columns

To select more than one row or column, click on a row or column heading. Hold down the left mouse button and drag to select adjacent rows or columns.

Selecting an entire worksheet

Click the Sheet Letter button:

A magnified view of the Sheet Letter button

Formulas - an overview

Formulas are cell entries which define how other values relate to each other.

As a very simple example, consider the following:

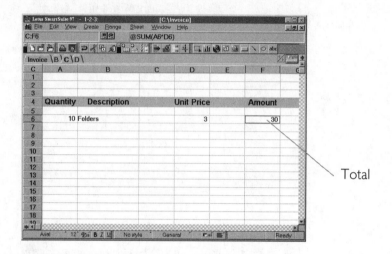

Total

'@' tells 1-2-3 that what follows is a formula; 'SUM(A6*D6)' tells 1-2-3 to multiply the contents of cells A6 and D6 and display the result.

Here, a cell has been defined which returns the product of the cells A6 and D6. Obviously, in this instance you could insert the total easily enough yourself because the individual values are so small, and because we're only dealing with a small number of cells. But what happens if the cell values are larger and/or more numerous, or – more to the point – if they're liable to change frequently?

The answer is to insert a formula which carries out the necessary calculation automatically.

If you look at the Contents box in the illustration, you'll see the formula which does this:

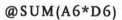

@SUM(A6*D6)

Many 1-2-3 formulas are much more complex than this, but the principles remain the same.

Inserting a formula

Arguments (e.g. cell references) relating to formulas and functions are always contained in brackets.

Functions (see page 84 for more information) are prefixed with @.

Formulas in 1-2-3 contain permutations of the following:

- an operand (cell reference, e.g. B4)

- a function (e.g. the summation function, SUM)

- an arithmetical operator (+, -, /, * and ^)

- logical operators (<, >, <=, >=, = and <>)

1-2-3 supports a very wide range of functions organised into numerous categories. For more information on how to insert functions, see the 'Using the Function Selector' topic.

The mathematical operators are (in the order in which they appear in the bulleted list above): *plus, minus, divide, multiply* and *exponentiation*.

The comparison operators are (in the order in which they appear in the list): *less than, greater than, less than or equal to, greater than or equal to, equals* and *not equal to.*

There are two ways to enter formulas:

Entering a formula directly into the cell
Click the cell in which you want to insert a formula. Then type it in – don't forget to surround the argument in brackets. For instance, to add cells H18 and I23, type:

(H18+I23)

When you've finished, press Return.

Entering a formula into the Contents box
Click the cell in which you want to insert a formula. Then click in the Contents box. Type in your formula. When you've finished, press Return or do the following:

Click here

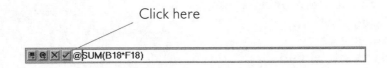

Using the Function Selector

HANDY TIP

The SUM component of the formula mentioned in the 'Formulas - an overview' topic is a function.

Functions are pre-defined tools which accomplish specific tasks. These tasks are often calculations; occasionally, however, they're more generalised (e.g. some functions simply return dates and/or times). In effect, functions replace one or more formulas.

1-2-3 provides a special tool to help ensure that you enter functions correctly. This is useful for the following reasons:

- 1-2-3 provides so many functions, it's convenient to apply them from a centralised source

- it's essential that functions are entered with the correct syntax

Functions can only be used in formulas.

Inserting a function with the Function Selector

At the relevant point in the process of inserting a formula, click the Function Selector button to the left of the Function bar:

     Function Selector button

HANDY TIP

1-2-3 organises its functions under convenient headings (e.g. Calendar, Information, Financial and Text). If you want to display specific functions in this dialog, click the arrow to the right of the Category field (before you carry out steps 2 & 3) and choose a category.

Now do the following:

Click here

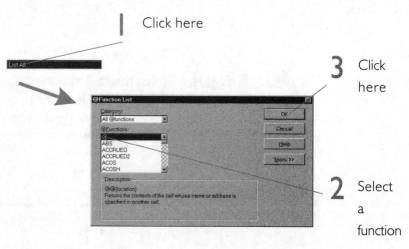

3 Click here

2 Select a function

Amending row/column sizes

Sooner or later, you'll find it necessary to change the width of rows or columns. This necessity arises when there is too much data in cells to display adequately. You can enlarge or shrink single or multiple rows/columns.

Changing row height

To change one row's height, click the row heading. If you want to change multiple rows, hold down Ctrl and click the appropriate extra headings. Then place the mouse pointer over the line located just under the row heading(s); it changes to a cross. Hold down the left mouse button and drag the line up or down to decrease or increase the height of the row(s) respectively. Release the mouse button to confirm the operation.

1-2-3 has a useful 'best fit' feature. Simply double-click the line below the selected row headings, or to the right of selected column headings, to have the rows or columns adjust themselves automatically to their textual content. Or hold down one Shift key as you double-click to have the rows or columns adjust to numerical content.

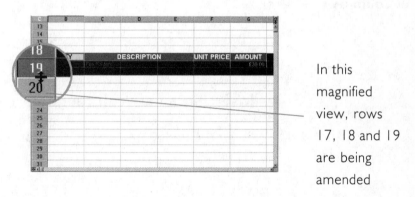

In this magnified view, rows 17, 18 and 19 are being amended

Changing column widths

To change one column's width, click the column heading. If you want to change multiple columns, hold down Ctrl and click the appropriate extra headings. Then place the mouse pointer over the line located just to the right of the column heading(s); it changes to a cross. Hold down the left mouse button and drag the line right or left to widen or narrow the column(s) respectively.

Release the mouse button to confirm the operation.

Inserting cells, rows or columns

You can insert additional cells, rows or columns into worksheets.

Inserting a new row or column

First, select one or more rows above which you want the new row(s) inserted. Or select one or more columns to the left of which you want the new column(s) inserted. Now pull down the Range menu and click Insert Rows or Insert Columns. 1-2-3 inserts the new row(s) or column(s) immediately.

If you select more than one row or column, 1-2-3 inserts the equivalent number of new rows or columns.

An extract of a worksheet. Here, four new rows are being added

Inserting a new cell range

Select the range where you want to insert the new cells. Pull down the Range menu and click Insert. Now carry out steps 1-3 below:

Click Rows or Columns

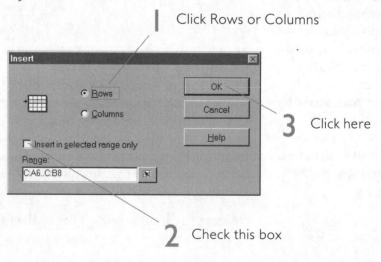

3 Click here

2 Check this box

Fill by Example

1-2-3 lets you insert data series automatically. This is a very useful and time-saving feature. Look at the illustration below:

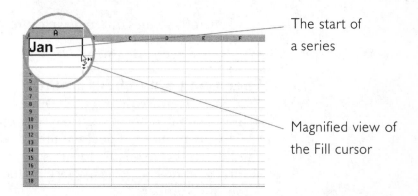

The start of a series

Magnified view of the Fill cursor

If you wanted to insert month names in successive cells in column A, you could do so manually. But there's a much easier way. You can use 1-2-3's Fill by Example feature.

You can also work with the following series types: numbers (e.g. 1, 3, 5, 7); letters (e.g. A, B, C, D) and days of the week.

HANDY TIP

Using Fill by Example to create a series

Type in the first element(s) of the series in consecutive cells. Select the cells you want to fill. Then position the mouse pointer over the bottom right-hand corner of the last cell (the pointer changes – see the illustration above). Hold down the left mouse button and drag over the cells into which you want to extend the series (in the example here, over A2..A12). When you release the mouse button, 1-2-3 extrapolates the initial entry or entries into the appropriate series.

The completed series

Changing number formats

1-2-3 lets you apply formatting enhancements to cells and their contents. You can:

- specify a number format

- customise the font, type size and style of contents

- specify cell alignment

Specifying a number format

You can customise the way cell contents (e.g. numbers and dates/times) display in 1-2-3. For example, you can often specify the number of decimal places which numbers should display. Available formats are organised under several general categories. These include: Currency, Date, Time and Number.

Select the cells whose contents you want to customise. Pull down the Range menu and click Range Properties. Now do the following:

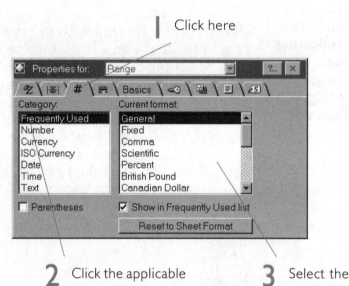

Click here

**Re step 3 –
the options
you can
choose
from vary according
to the category
chosen.**

2 Click the applicable
category

3 Select the
relevant format

Changing fonts and attributes

1-2-3 lets you carry out the following actions on cell contents (numbers and/or text):

*   apply a new font and/or type size

*   apply a font attribute – for most fonts, you can choose from: Normal, Italic, Bold or Underline

*   apply a colour

Amending the appearance of cell contents

Select the cell(s) whose contents you want to reformat. Pull down the Style menu and click Font & Attributes. Now follow any of steps 1-4, as appropriate. Finally, carry out step 5.

1 Click here
2 Click the font you want to use
3 Enter the type size you need

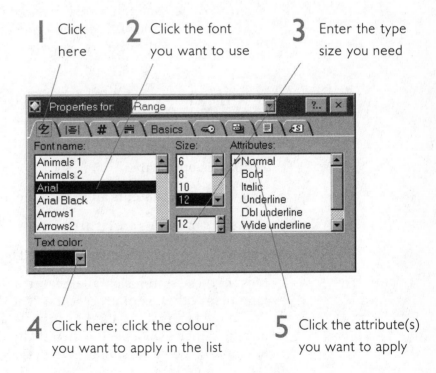

4 Click here; click the colour you want to apply in the list
5 Click the attribute(s) you want to apply

Cell alignment (1)

By default, 1-2-3 aligns text to the left of cells, and numbers to the right. However, if you want you can change this.

You can specify alignment under two broad headings: Horizontal and Vertical.

Horizontal alignment
The main options are:

General	the default (see above)
Left	contents are aligned from the left
Center	contents are centred
Right	contents are aligned from the right
Evenly Spaced	contents are separated by spaces so that they fill the cell – see the excerpted cell in the example below:

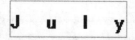 A cell with Evenly Spaced alignment

Vertical alignment
Available options are:

Top	cell contents align with the top of the cell(s)
Center	contents are centred
Bottom	contents align with the cell bottom

Most of these settings parallel features found in WordPro (and many other word processors). The difference, however, lies in the fact that 1-2-3 has to align data within the bounds of cells rather than a page. When it aligns text, it often needs to employ its own version of text wrap. See 'Cell alignment (2)' for more information on this.

You can also specify an orientation for cell contents – see 'Cell alignment (2)'.

Cell alignment (2)

Other alignment features you can set are orientation and text wrap.

Orientation controls the direction of text flow within cells; there are several available options, expressed visually in the Orientation field in the Alignment dialog.

When the Wrap text option is selected, 1-2-3 – instead of overflowing any surplus text into adjacent cells to the right – forces it onto separate lines within the host cell.

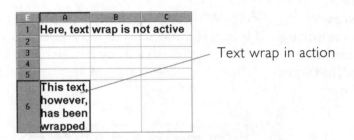

Text wrap in action

Customising cell alignment

Select the cell(s) whose contents you want to realign. Pull down the Range menu and click Range Properties. Carry out step 1 below. Now follow steps 2-4, as appropriate.

Re step 4 – choose an orientation from the following drop-down list:

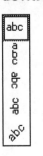

Click here

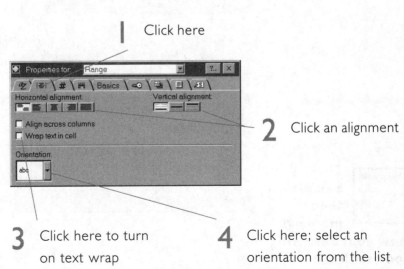

2 Click an alignment

3 Click here to turn on text wrap

4 Click here; select an orientation from the list

Using the Gallery

1-2-3 provides a shortcut to the formatting of worksheet data: the Gallery.

The Gallery consists of 14 pre-defined formatting schemes. These incorporate specific excerpts from several of the formatting options that were discussed earlier; additionally, a few incorporate three-dimensional components for increased visual effect. You can apply any of these schemes (and their associated formatting) to selected cell ranges with just a few mouse clicks.

The **Gallery works with most arrangements of data. However, some may require a certain amount of manual adjustment first...**

Applying preset formatting

First, select the cell range you want to apply an automatic format to. Pull down the Range menu and click Range Properties. Now carry out steps 1-4 below:

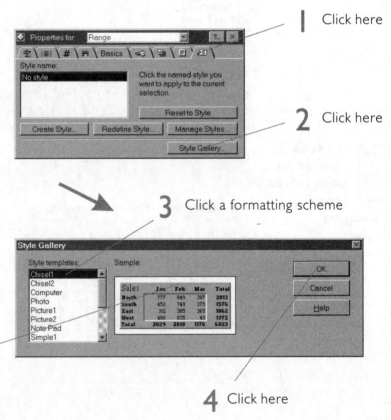

Click here

Click here

Click a formatting scheme

Click here

The **Sample field previews how your data will look with the specified template.**

Find operations

1-2-3 lets you search for and jump to text or numbers (in short, any information) in your worksheets. This is a particularly useful feature when worksheets become large and complex, as they almost invariably do.

You can specify whether 1-2-3 looks in:

- cells which contain text ('labels')

- cells which don't contain formulas

- cells which contain text *and* those which contain formulas

- all open worksheets (or simply a pre-selected cell range – see the second tip)

Searching for data

Pull down the Edit menu and click Find & Replace. Now carry out step 1 below, then either or both of steps 2 and 3. Finally, carry out step 4.

| Type in the data you want to find

4 Click here

HANDY TIP

If you want a case-specific search, select Case in the Match section before you follow step 4.

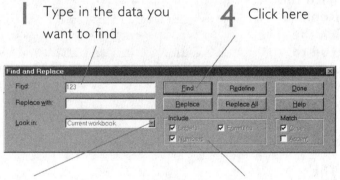

2 Click here; select a search definition in the list

3 Define the types of cells searched

Find-and-replace operations

When you search for data, you can also have 1-2-3 replace it with something else. You can have this done automatically, or you can have 1-2-3 request your confirmation before making the exchange.

As with find operations, you can specify whether 1-2-3 looks in cells which contain text, cells which contain formulas, or both. You can also have 1-2-3 search through all active worksheets, or through selected cell ranges.

Running a find-and-replace operation

Pull down the Edit menu and click Find & Replace. Carry out steps 1 and 2, then 3 and/or 4, as appropriate. Follow step 5 to replace only *one* flagged instance of the search data (repeat as often as necessary). Alternatively, follow step 6 to replace *all* instances.

1 Type in the data you want to find

2 Type in the replacement data

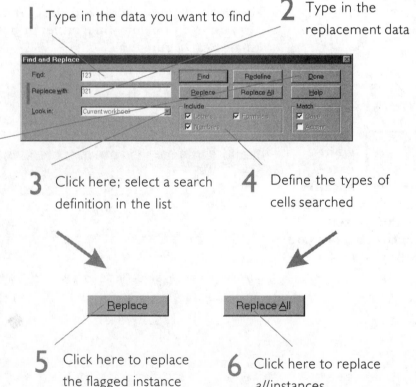

HANDY TIP

When you've finished with the Find and Replace dialog, click the Done button to close it:

3 Click here; select a search definition in the list

4 Define the types of cells searched

REMEMBER

The buttons shown on the right are excerpts from the Find and Replace dialog.

5 Click here to replace the flagged instance

6 Click here to replace *all* instances

Charting (1)

1-2-3 has comprehensive charting capabilities. You can have it convert selected data into its visual equivalent. To do this, 1-2-3 offers a wide number of chart formats and sub-formats.

Creating a chart

Select the cells you want 1-2-3 to convert into a chart. Pull down the Create menu and click Chart. The cursor changes to:

Hold down the left mouse button and drag to define the area into which you want the new chart inserted.

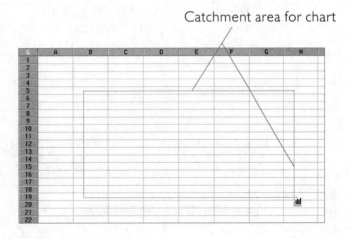

Catchment area for chart

When you release the button, 1-2-3 inserts the chart.

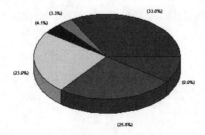

Charting (2)

By default, 1-2-3 creates simple bar charts. However, you can easily apply a new chart type if you want.

You can choose from 12 overall chart types. These include:

- Line

- Area

- Pie

- 3D versions of the above

- Radar

Many of these are further divided into sub-types.

Applying a new chart type

To change the chart type, do the following. Select the chart by clicking it. Pull down the Chart menu and click Chart Type. Now do the following:

Click a chart type

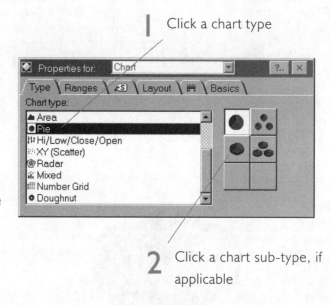

REMEMBER

The 1-2-3 sub-types provide a lot of variety. Below are the sub-types associated with the Bar type:

2 Click a chart sub-type, if applicable

Page setup issues

1-2-3 lets you set page setup options within an overall Preview screen (for how to use the Preview component, see pages 98 & 99).

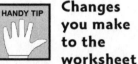

Changes you make to the worksheet layout are mirrored in the Preview window:

Re step 2 – you can centre-print data vertically, horizontally or both.

Making sure your worksheets print with the correct page setup can be a complex issue, for the simple reason that most worksheets become very extensive with the passage of time (so large, in fact, that in the normal course of things they won't fit onto a single page).

Page setup features you can customise include:

- the paper orientation

- scaling

- margins (Top, Bottom, Left and Right)

- the centring of data

Setting page options

Pull down the File menu and click Preview & Page Setup. Now do the following, as appropriate:

1 Click an orientation   2 Click a centre alignment

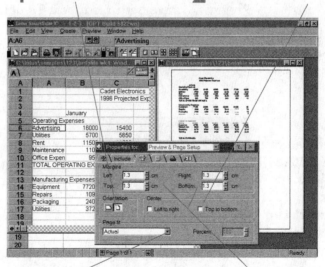

3 Click here; choose a scaling option

4 Adjust the relevant margin settings

Launching Dynamic Preview

1-2-3 provides a special view mode called Dynamic Preview. This displays the active worksheet exactly as it will look when printed. Alongside this is a window showing the normal worksheet view. Use Dynamic Preview as a final check just before you begin printing.

You can perform the following actions from within Dynamic Preview:

- move from page to page

- zoom in or out on the active page

- display more than one page

- adjust Page Setup options (see page 97)

- begin printing

Launching Dynamic Preview

Pull down the File menu and click Preview & Page Setup. The Preview window now launches, together with the Preview & Page Setup Infobox. To determine which worksheet sections are previewed, carry out step 1 below, then 2-3, as appropriate:

To determine the paper size, click this tab:

Then click the arrow to the right of the Paper size field. In the list which launches, select the paper size you want to use.

Click here

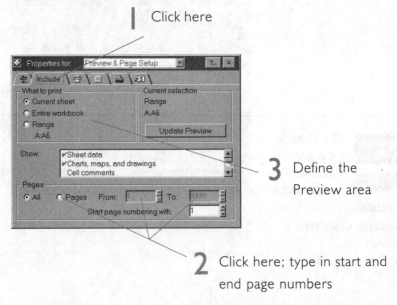

3 Define the Preview area

2 Click here; type in start and end page numbers

Using Dynamic Preview

All of the operations you can undertake in Dynamic Preview can be accessed from the overhead SmartIcons.

Do any of the following, as appropriate:

To previous page | Displays one page | Displays 9 pages | Closes the active window

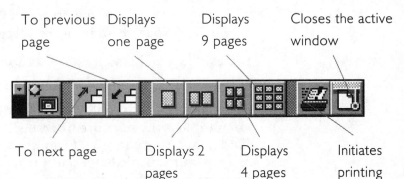

To next page | Displays 2 pages | Displays 4 pages | Initiates printing

To zoom in or out in the Dynamic Preview window, position the mouse cursor in the appropriate position and left-click.

To close the Dynamic Preview window, click the ⊠ button.

To move to a part of your worksheet which isn't currently visible, use the scroll bars.

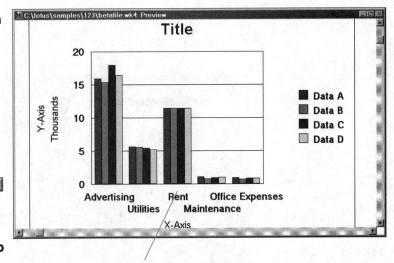

The Dynamic Preview window showing a chart

Printing worksheet data

1-2-3 lets you specify:

• the number of copies you want printed

• which pages (or page ranges) you want printed

• whether you want the print run restricted to cells you selected before initiating printing

You can 'mix and match' these, as appropriate.

Starting a print run

Open the file which contains the data you want to print. If you want to print an entire worksheet, click the relevant divider tab. Alternatively, if you need to print a specific cell range within a worksheet, select it. Then pull down the File menu and click Print. Do any of steps 1-3. Then carry out step 4 to begin printing:

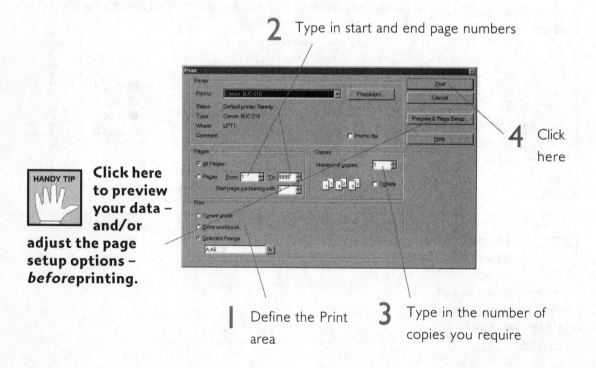

2 Type in start and end page numbers

HANDY TIP **Click here to preview your data – and/or adjust the page setup options – *before*printing.**

4 Click here

| Define the Print area

3 Type in the number of copies you require

Approach

This chapter gives you the fundamentals of using Approach. You'll learn how to work with data and formulas, and how to move around through databases. You'll also learn how to locate data, and apply formatting to make it more visually effective. Finally, you'll customise page layout/printing.

Covers

The Approach screen

Below is a detailed illustration of a typical Approach screen.

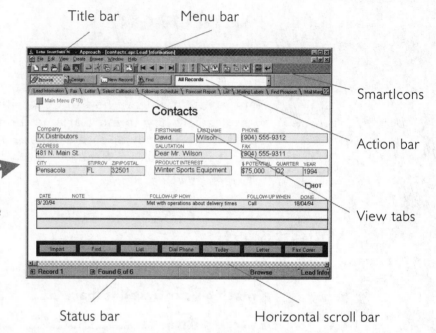

Title bar   Menu bar

SmartIcons

Action bar

View tabs

This is a database form (it displays one record at a time). For more information on forms, see the 'Using Browse mode' topic later.

Status bar   Horizontal scroll bar

Some of these – e.g. the Title and Menu bars – are standard to just about all programs which run under Windows. Other components can be hidden at will.

Specifying which screen components display

Pull down the File menu; click User Setup, Approach Preferences. Then do the following:

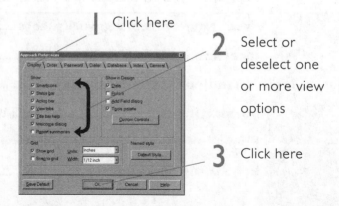

Click here

2 Select or deselect one or more view options

3 Click here

Creating your first database (1)

We saw in Section One how to create new blank documents in all four SmartSuite modules. Approach, however, has certain refinements. We'll look at the process in more detail here.

To create a new database from within Approach, pull down the File menu and click New Database. Do the following:

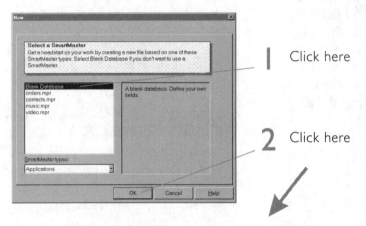

1 Click here

2 Click here

3 Click here. In the drop-down list, click the drive/folder you want to host the database

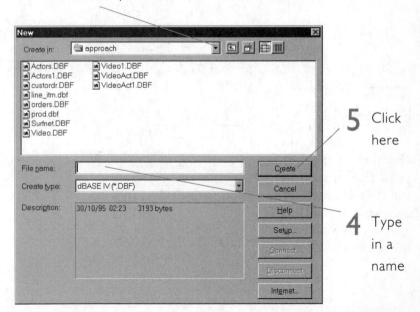

5 Click here

4 Type in a name

Creating your first database (2)

The next stage is to define the fields you want your new database to have. Carry out step 1 below:

Type in a field name

In Approach, data is entered into individual fields. (For more information on fields, see the 'Entering data' topics.)

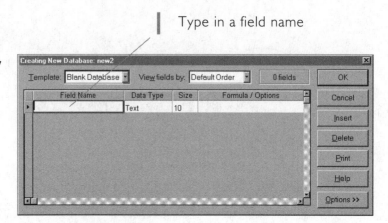

Now press Return. Repeat this procedure for as many fields as you need (you can, of course, add additional fields later, if required). The completed dialog will look something like this:

2 Click here

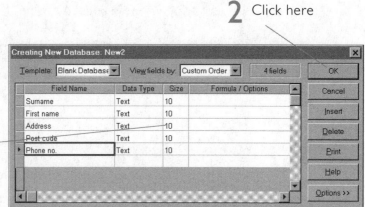

The entries in the Size column determine the size of the fields (and therefore how much information can be inserted). It's a good idea to increase the default now.

Follow step 2 when you've entered enough fields. Approach creates the new database.

Entering data (1)

When you've created a database, you can begin entering data immediately. You can enter the following basic data types:

- numbers

- text

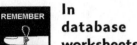

In database worksheets, records are shown as single rows. In forms, on the other hand, only one record displays on-screen at any given time. For more information on this, see the 'Using Browse mode' topic later.

- functions

- formulas (combinations of numbers, text and functions)

You enter data into 'fields'. Fields are organised into 'records'. Records are whole units of related information.

To understand this, we'll take a specific example. In an address book, the categories under which information is entered (e.g. 'Surname', 'Address', 'Phone No.') are fields, while each person whose details are entered into the database constitutes one record. The next illustration (this is the database we created in 'Creating your first database') shows this:

This is a worksheet. Database worksheets are suitable for the mass insertion of data; if applicable (it isn't here), more than 1 record is visible at a time. However, you can also enter data in forms.

Fields

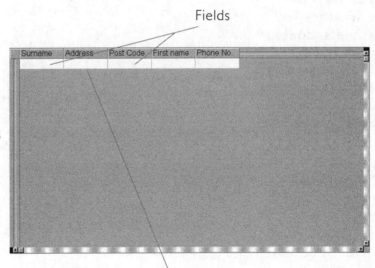

All five fields constitute one record here

Entering data (2)

You must be in Browse mode to enter or amend data (see the 'Using Browse mode' topic).

You can enter data *directly* into a database field. You can do this in both forms and worksheets (but see the tip).

In the illustration below, data is being entered into a form:

Click a field, then begin entering data

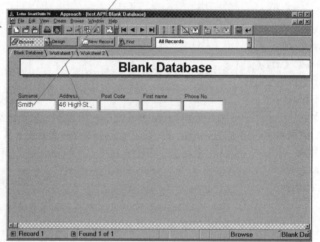

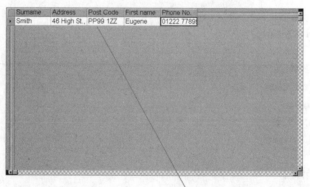

To modify existing data, click in the relevant field. Make the necessary alterations and/or additions, then press Enter. For more accuracy in worksheets, double-click a field (this places the insertion point inside existing data) then amend it as above.

Press Enter to confirm the operation. Repeat this procedure for as many fields as necessary.

The completed record viewed in a worksheet

Using Browse mode

There is another way in which you can interact with Approach: Design mode. This mostly relates to forms rather than worksheets, and will be discussed in later topics.

Most of your work in Approach will be done in Browse mode. Browse mode is used for editing data; you do this by using two further database components: forms and worksheets.

Forms

Forms display only one record at a time, while presenting it in a way that is more visual and therefore easier on the eye. The form is the underlying database layout, which you can customise in Design mode. In many circumstances, Forms provide the best way to interact with your database.

Worksheets

Worksheets present data in a grid structure reminiscent of 1-2-3, with the columns denoting fields and the rows individual records. Pictures and many formatting components do not display. Use worksheets for *bulk* data entry.

This is the form component of a database created with the Video and Actor SmartMaster.

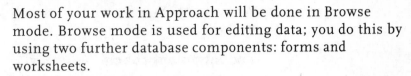

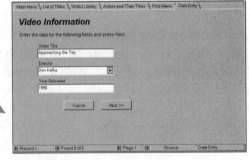

And this is a worksheet from the same database.

LAST_NAME	FIRST_NAME	BIRTHDATE	MOVIE_TITL	YEARRELEAS	FindVariable	FInd
Gregory	Anthony	15/02/40	The Longest Hour	1957		
Longely	Andrea	01/03/70	Wildflowers	1994		
Jones	Sarah	19/10/75	The Last Dance	1993		
Kane	Mark	03/01/77	Wednesday	1980		
Lamond	Tina	05/04/67	Approaching the Top	1990		
Manzanita	Antonio	08/09/46	Lotus Blossom	1963		
Spencer	Michael	03/03/50	Approaching the Top	1990		
Taylor	Steve	08/04/77	Approaching the Top	1990		
Yen	Mark	24/11/65	The Last Dance	1993		
Yen	Mark	24/11/65	Wednesday	1980		
Yamamoto	Toshiro	05/03/32	Lotus Blossom	1963		
Yamamoto	Toshiro	05/03/32	The Longest Hour	1957		
Baker	Joseph	15/12/77	Photo Shoot	1995		
Kane	Mark	03/01/77	Photo Shoot	1995		
Lamond	Tina	05/04/67	Going Downtown	1987		
Spencer	Michael	03/03/50	Going Downtown	1987		
Spencer	Michael	03/03/50	Wildflowers	1994		

Switching between modes

You can use three methods to switch between Browse and Design modes.

The menu approach

Pull down the View menu and do the following:

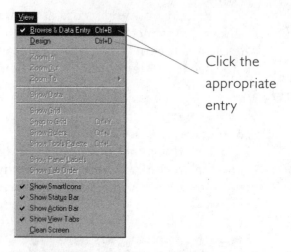

Click the
appropriate
entry

The Action bar approach

Make sure the Action bar is visible. (If it isn't, pull down the View menu and click Show Action Bar.) Now click one of the following:

Click here to enter Design Mode

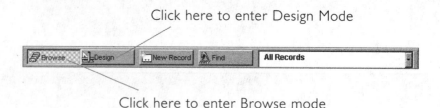

Click here to enter Browse mode

The keyboard approach

Use any of the following combinations:

Ctrl+B   Browse mode

Ctrl+D   Design mode

Moving around in databases (1)

Like worksheets in 1-2-3, databases can quickly become very large.

Approach provides several techniques you can use to find your way around.

Using the scroll bars
Use any of the following methods:

1. To scroll quickly to another record in worksheets, drag the vertical scroll box along the scroll bar until it's visible. To reach another field in forms, drag the horizontal scroll box until it's visible.

2. To move one window to the left or right (in both worksheets and forms), click to the left or right of the scroll box in the horizontal scroll bar.

3. To move one window up or down (in both worksheets and forms), click above or below the scroll box in the vertical scroll bar.

4. To move left or right by one field in worksheets, click the arrows in the horizontal scroll bar.

Scroll boxes

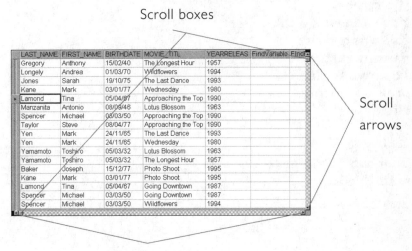

Scroll arrows

Scroll arrows

Moving around in databases (2)

Using the keyboard

You can use the following techniques:

1.   In worksheets, use the cursor keys to move one field left, right, up or down. Or press Tab to move to the adjoining field on the right (note that Shift+Tab reverses the direction).

2.   In forms, press Tab to move to the next field (note that Shift+Tab reverses the direction).

3.   In forms and worksheets, press Ctrl+Home to move to the first record in the open database, or Ctrl+End to move to the last.

4.   In worksheets, press Page Up or Page Down to move up or down by one screen.

5.   In forms, press Page Down to view the next record, or Page Up to view the previous one.

This is the Record button in the Status bar at the base of the screen. You can also do the following in the Record button: To move to the previous record, click:

To move to the next record, click:

Using the Go to Record dialog

Approach provides a special dialog that you can use to specify which record you want to view. Do the following:

Click here

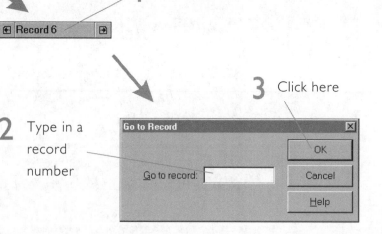

1

2   Type in a record number

3   Click here

Using Zoom

You can only use Zoom in Design mode.

The ability to vary the level of magnification in Approach is very useful. Sometimes, it's helpful to 'zoom out' (i.e. decrease the magnification) so that you can take an overview; at other times, you'll need to 'zoom in' (increase the magnification) to work in greater detail. SmartSuite makes this process easy and convenient.

You can change magnification levels in Approach:

- from within the View menu

- by using the Zoom button in the Status bar

Using the View menu

In Design mode, pull down the View menu. Now do the following:

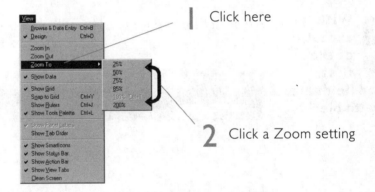

Click here

2 Click a Zoom setting

Using the Zoom button

Do the following:

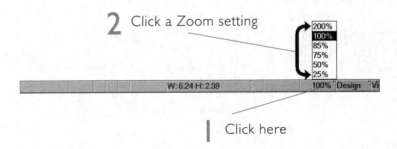

2 Click a Zoom setting

Click here

Selection techniques in worksheets

Before you can carry out any editing operations on fields or records in Approach, you have to select them first. The available selection techniques vary according to whether you're currently using worksheets or forms.

Follow any of the techniques below:

To select a single field   simply click in it

To select multiple fields   click the field in the top left-hand corner of the range you want to select; hold down the mouse button and drag over the fields you want to highlight. Release the mouse button.

To select one record   click the record header

To select multiple records   hold down Shift as you click the record headers

With the exception of the first, selected fields are filled with black.

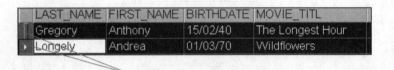

LAST_NAME	FIRST_NAME	BIRTHDATE	MOVIE_TITL
Gregory	Anthony	15/02/40	The Longest Hour
Longely	Andrea	01/03/70	Wildflowers

Record headers

To select all data within the active worksheet   do the following:

HANDY TIP

To select all columns and rows (but not the data), click here again.

LA AME	FIRST_NAME	BIRTHDATE	MOVIE_TITL	YEARRELEAS	FindVariable	Fin
	Anthony	15/02/40	The Longest Hour	1957		
Gly	Andrea	01/03/70	Wildflowers	1994		
es	Sarah	19/10/75	The Last Dance	1993		
Kane	Mark	03/01/77	Wednesday	1980		
Lamond	Tina	05/04/67	Approaching the Top	1990		
Manzanita	Antonio	08/09/46	Lotus Blossom	1963		
Spencer	Michael	03/03/50	Approaching the Top	1990		
Taylor	Steve	08/04/77	Approaching the Top	1990		
Yen	Mark	24/11/65	The Last Dance	1993		
Yen	Mark	24/11/65	Wednesday	1980		
Yamamoto	Toshiro	05/03/32	Lotus Blossom	1963		
Yamamoto	Toshiro	05/03/32	The Longest Hour	1957		
Baker	Joseph	15/12/77	Photo Shoot	1995		
Kane	Mark	03/01/77	Photo Shoot	1995		
Lamond	Tina	05/04/67	Going Downtown	1987		
Spencer	Michael	03/03/50	Going Downtown	1987		
Spencer	Michael	03/03/50	Wildflowers	1994		

Click here

Selection techniques in forms

Using the mouse

To select a single field   simply click in it

To select multiple fields   hold down Shift as you click in successive fields (you must be in Design mode to do this)

Note that some of the techniques discussed here (they're clearly marked) will only work in Design mode.

To select one record   use the Record button in the Status bar (for how to do this, see the 'Moving around in databases (2)' topic earlier)

To select inserted pictures   In Design mode, hold down Shift as you click on successive pictures

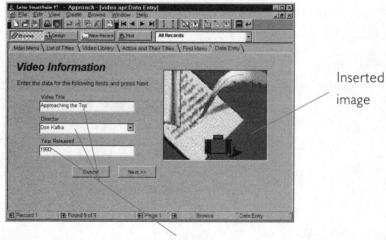

Inserted image

Fields

Using the keyboard

To select a record   Press Page Up or Page Down until the record you want is displayed

Formulas - an overview

You can insert formulas into Approach databases, but only in worksheets. Formulas in Approach work in (very broadly) the same way as in 1-2-3. However, there are certain stipulations:

- you can only insert formulas into whole columns (rather than into individual fields)

- as a result of the above, formulas can only apply to data in rows (records), although you can exclude specific fields

Look at the next illustration:

In Approach, you can total rows (records)...

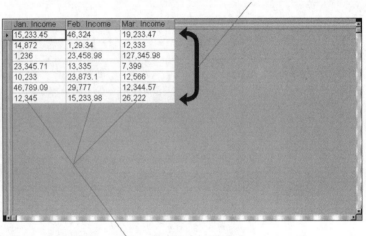

Jan. Income	Feb. Income	Mar. Income
15,233.45	46,324	19,233.47
14,872	1,29.34	12,333
1,236	23,458.98	127,345.98
23,345.71	13,335	7,399
10,233	23,873.1	12,566
46,789.09	29,777	12,344.57
12,345	15,233,98	26,222

...but not individual fields (columns)

You can, for example, insert a column which automatically totals the data in all 7 rows/records (or only the data in specific fields within all the records), but it isn't possible to total the individual columns.

Inserting a formula (1)

As in 1-2-3, Approach formulas are usually followed by a permutation of the following:

- one or more operands (in the case of Approach, field names)

- a function (e.g. AVG – returns the Average)

- an arithmetical operator (e.g. +, -, /, * and ^)

Approach supports a very wide assortment of functions. For brief information on how to insert functions, refer to the 'Inserting a formula (2)' topic.

The arithmetical operators are (in the order in which they appear in the bulleted list above):

plus, minus, divide, multiply and *exponential.*

Formulas can only be entered in one (highly specific) two-stage process.

Creating a formula column

In a worksheet, move the mouse pointer over the header of the column to the right of which you want the formula column inserted. The pointer changes to a wedge:

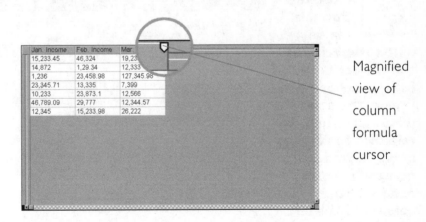

Magnified view of column formula cursor

Left-click once.

Inserting a formula (2)

HANDY TIP

When the red cross disappears from the flag, the syntax of your formula is workable (though not necessarily complete).

HANDY TIP

Re step 2 - to enter a function instead, click an entry in this field:
Complete the syntax in the Formula box, then follow step 3.

BEWARE

If you close the Formula dialog without specifying the correct formula/ function, Approach inserts the new (empty) column. To relaunch the dialog, move the mouse pointer over the header of the column to the left and click the wedge. Complete the dialog as appropriate.

The next stage in inserting a formula is the completion of the Formula dialog.

Carry out steps 1 and 2 below as often as necessary. (In this particular example, you need to carry out step 1 in respect of all three fields, and step 2 twice). Finally, carry out step 3 when you've finished:

1 Double-click a field

3 Click here

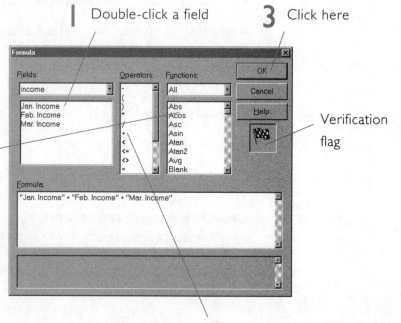

Verification flag

2 Double-click an operator

After step 3, Approach inserts the formula column:

Jan. Income	Feb. Income	Mar. Income	
15,233.45	46,324	19,233.47	80790.92
14,872	1,29.34	12,333	27334.34
1,236	23,458.98	127,345.98	152040.96
23,345.71	13,335	7,399	44079.71
10,233	23,873.1	12,566	46672.1
46,789.09	29,777	12,344.57	88910.66
12,345	15,233.98	26,222	53800.98

Formula column

Creating new forms

Approach lets you create new forms in your databases.

Pull down the Create menu and click Form. Now do the following:

1   Name the new form   2   Click a layout

HANDY TIP **The Sample Form field provides a preview of what your form will look like.**

3   Click here; select a style   4   Click here

5   Click a field

REMEMBER **Repeat steps 5 & 6 for as many fields as you want to add to the new form. Then carry out step 7.**

7   Click here

6   Click here

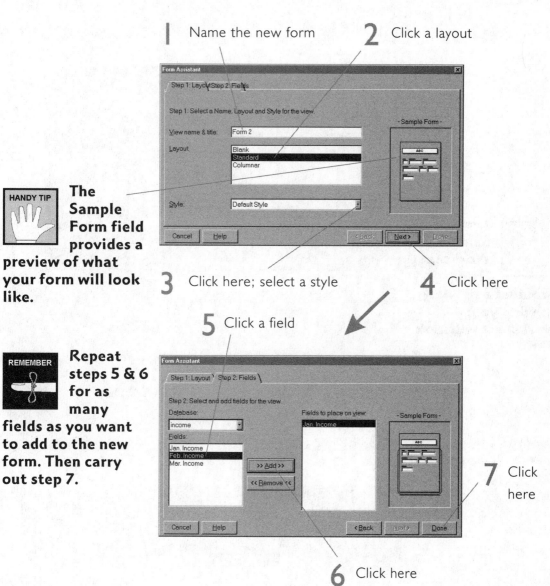

Creating new worksheets

Approach lets you create new worksheets in your databases.

Pull down the Create menu and click Worksheet. Now do the following:

1 Click a field   **2** Click here

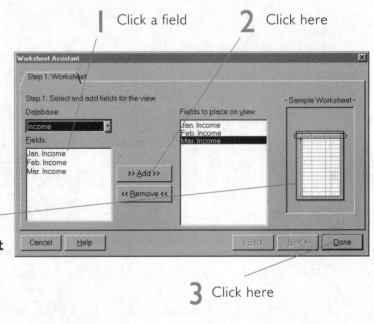

HANDY TIP **The Sample Worksheet field** provides a preview of what your worksheet will look like.

3 Click here

Approach creates and inserts the new worksheet.

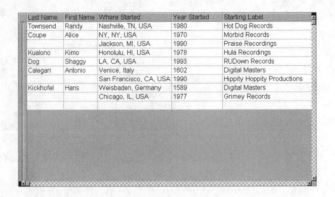

Creating/inserting new fields

You can add one or more blank fields to the active database, from within forms (in Design mode) or worksheets (in Browse or Design mode). Once created, fields can be inserted into the database.

Pull down the Create menu and click Field Definition. Do the following:

HANDY TIP

When you follow step 1, Approach creates another blank field below the new one. Ignore this unless you want to create a further field.

2 Click here

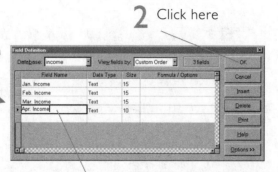

Click the blank field at the base of the current fields; type in a name for the new field

3 Click the new field; drag it to where you want it placed

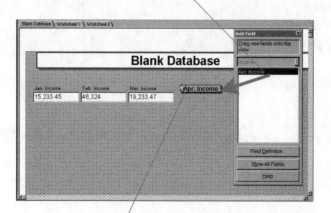

4 Release the button

Inserting a record

You can add blank records to the active database from within forms or worksheets (but not if you're working with a form in Design mode).

Refer to the Action bar at the top of the screen and do the following:

HANDY TIP

There's a keyboard shortcut you can use here: simply press Ctrl+N.

Click here

Approach now creates and inserts the new record.

The illustration below shows a new record in a form.

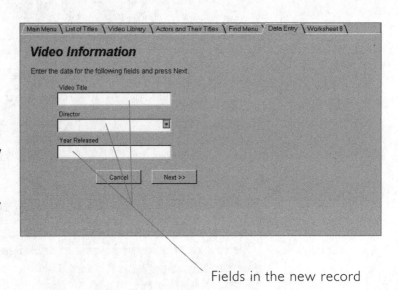

REMEMBER

If you want to abort new record creation before you've entered any data, simply press Esc.

Fields in the new record

Complete the new fields in the usual way.

Amending record/field sizes

Sooner or later, you'll find it necessary to change the dimensions of fields or records within worksheets. This necessity arises when there is too much data to display adequately. You can enlarge or shrink all records within a worksheet, or individual columns.

Changing record height

To change the height of all records within a worksheet, move the mouse pointer over any record header. The pointer changes to a double-headed cross. Click and hold down the left mouse button; drag the records down to enlarge them, or up to shrink them.

These are row headers:

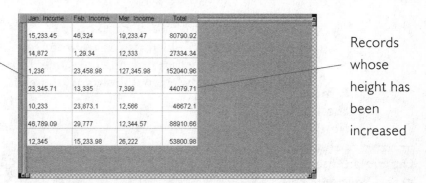

Records whose height has been increased

Changing field widths

To change one field/column's width, click the header. If you want to change multiple fields, hold down Shift and click the appropriate extra headers. Then move the mouse pointer over the left or right header edge. Drag inwards to shrink the fields, or outwards to enlarge them.

Jan. Income	Feb. Income	Mar. Income	Total
15,233.45	46,324	19,233.47	80790.92
14,872	1,29.34	12,333	27334.34
1,236	23,458.98	127,345.98	152040.96
23,345.71	13,335	7,399	44079.71
10,233	23,873.1	12,566	46672.1
46,789.09	29,777	12,344.57	88910.66
12,345	15,233.98	26,222	53800.98

Column headers

These columns have been resized

Changing fonts and attributes

In forms in Design mode, Approach lets you carry out the following actions on field contents (numbers, text or combinations of both):

- apply a new font

- apply a new type size

- apply an alignment

- apply a font attribute (*Italic,* **Bold**, <u>Underlining</u> or ~~Strikethrough)~~

- apply a colour

Amending field contents

Select the field/data you want to reformat. Pull down the Field Object menu and click Object Properties. Carry out step 1 below. Now follow any of steps 2-6, as appropriate.

HANDY TIP

If more than one field is selected, the Field Object menu becomes the **Multiple Objects menu.**

1 Click this tab   3 Enter a type size

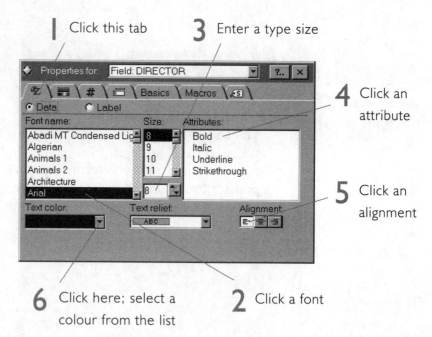

4 Click an attribute

5 Click an alignment

6 Click here; select a colour from the list

2 Click a font

Bordering fields

The baseline is the imaginary line on which text (excluding 'descenders' - the lowest points of letters like p & q) sits:

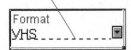

In forms in Design mode, you can define and customise a border around one or more fields (to select more than one field, hold down the Shift key as you click on them). You can specify:

• which sides are bordered

• whether you want the text baseline shown

• the border colour

• the border thickness

• a preset border style

Applying a field border

First, select the field/data you want to reformat. Pull down the Field Object menu and click Object Properties. Carry out step 1 below. Then follow steps 2-5, as appropriate:

If more than one field is selected, the Field Object menu becomes the Multiple Objects menu.

1 Ensure this tab is active

2 Click here; select a style from the list

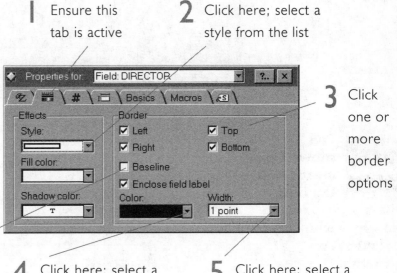

3 Click one or more border options

Click here: to display the text baseline.

4 Click here; select a colour from the list

5 Click here; select a width from the list

Shading fields

In forms in Design mode, you can apply the following to one or more fields:

• a fill colour

• a shadow colour

Applying a fill and/or shadow colour

First, select the field/data you want to reformat. Pull down the Field Object menu and click Object Properties. Carry out step 1 below. Then follow steps 2-4, as appropriate (both steps 2 and 3 lead to step 4):

HANDY TIP

If more than one field is selected, the Field Object menu becomes the Multiple Objects menu.

| Ensure this
tab is active

2 Click here; select a
colour from the list

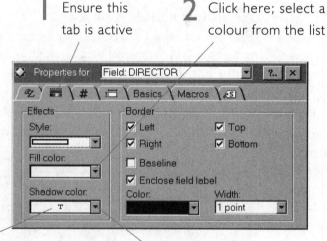

REMEMBER

The 'T' shown here means that the field fill is 'transparent': i.e. any background colour shows through.

3 Click here; select a colour from the list

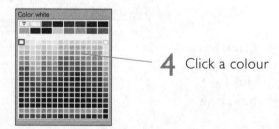

4 Click a colour

Find operations

You must be in Browse mode to carry out Find operations.

Approach lets you search for text and/or numbers in forms and worksheets. You can:

- limit the search to a specific selection

- (in forms) limit the search specifically to the active record

- make the search case-sensitive (e.g. searching for 'March' would not flag 'march')

- search for the whole field (e.g. searching for 'part' would not flag 'party' or 'partly')

Searching for data

This is the worksheet version of the Find & Replace Text dialog. It's slightly different when you launch it from within a form.

Pull down the Edit menu and click Find & Replace Text. Follow step 1 below. Carry out steps 2 and 3, if applicable. Now follow step 4. To find further instances of the search data, carry out step 5.

Type in the data you want to locate

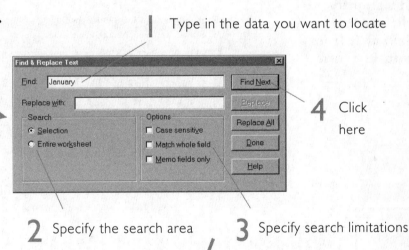

4 Click here

2 Specify the search area

3 Specify search limitations

To terminate a search operation at any time, simply click the Close button.

5 Click here

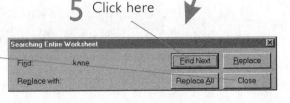

Find-and-replace operations

When you search for data, you can also – if you want – have Approach replace it with something else.

You must be in Browse mode to carry out find-and-replace operations.

Running a find-and-replace operation

In a form or worksheet, pull down the Edit menu and click Find & Replace Text. Follow steps 1 and 2 below. Carry out steps 3 and 4, if applicable. Now do *one* of the following:

• Follow step 5. When Approach locates the first search target, carry out step 7 to have it replaced. Approach finds the next instance automatically. Repeat step 7 as often as necessary.

• Carry out step 6 to have SmartSuite find *every* target and replace it automatically.

This is the worksheet version of the Find & Replace Text dialog. It's slightly different when you launch it from within a form.

1 Type in the data you want to locate

2 Type in the replacement data

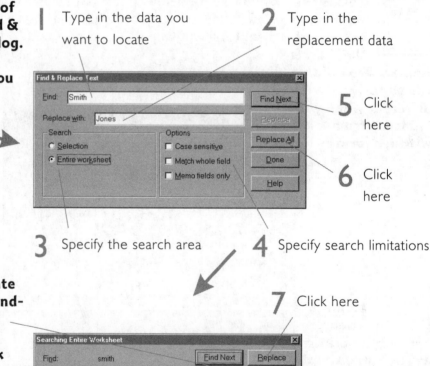

5 Click here

6 Click here

3 Specify the search area

4 Specify search limitations

7 Click here

To terminate a find-and-replace operation at any time, simply click the Close button.

Page setup - an overview

When you come to print out your database, it's important to ensure the page setup is correct. Luckily, SmartSuite makes this easy.

You can specify:

- the paper size

- the page orientation

- the page margins

- (in worksheets only) whether or not you want any of the following components printed:

    - a database title

    - the current date

    - page numbers

With the exception of the latter, you can do any of these from within forms or worksheets, but you must be in Design mode.

Note that when you change page setup parameters within a form or worksheet, the changes are not global: they only apply to the original form/worksheet.

Margin settings you can amend are:

- Top

- Bottom

- Left

- Right

Setting size/orientation options

Approach comes with 17 pre-defined paper types which you can apply to your databases, in either portrait (top-to-bottom) or landscape (sideways-on) orientation.

Portrait orientation

Landscape orientation

Applying a new page size/orientation

In Design mode, pull down the File menu and click Page Setup. Now carry out step 1 and/or 2 below. Finally, follow step 3:

Click here; select a page size from the list

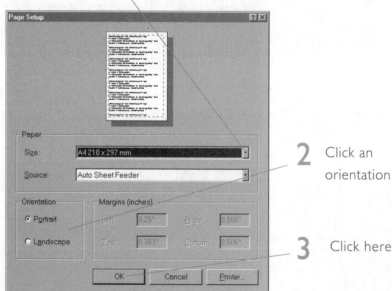

2 Click an orientation

3 Click here

Setting margin options

Approach lets you set a variety of margin settings. The illustration below shows the main ones:

Margin options can only be set from within forms, in Design mode.

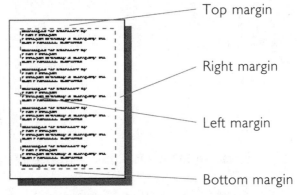

Top margin

Right margin

Left margin

Bottom margin

Applying new margins

In a form within Design mode, make sure no field is selected. Pull down the Form menu and click Form Properties. Do the following:

Ensure the Margins tab is active

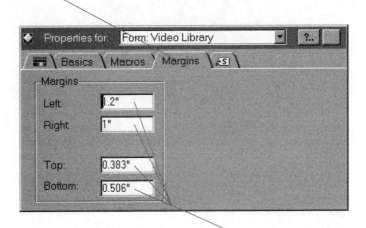

2 Type in new margin settings

Other page setup options

When you print out worksheets, they print as tables or lists. Because of this, Approach lets you:

- print out a heading, if you want, at the head of the page

- include the current date and/or page number at the base of the page (the date appears on the left, the number on the right)

You can specify the heading text on-the-fly (you don't have to insert it within the worksheet itself).

Setting title and date/number options

In a worksheet (in either Browse or Design modes), pull down the Worksheet menu and click Worksheet Properties. Now carry out steps 1-3 below, as appropriate:

Click here, then type in the heading you want to use

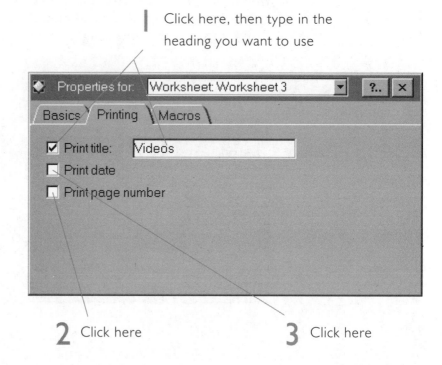

2 Click here   3 Click here

Print Preview

You can't use Print Preview to edit data or reformat fields. Use Browse and Design modes for these.

Approach provides a special view called Print Preview. Print Preview can be launched from within forms or worksheets, in Browse or Design modes, and indicates what your data will look like when printed out.

By default, Print Preview displays your data at a magnification of 85%. You can easily change this if you want by stepping up or down through predetermined zoom levels.

Use Print Preview for a final verification of your database before you print it.

Launching Print Preview
Pull down the File menu and click Print Preview.

Using Print Preview
In Print Preview, the mouse pointer changes to a magnifying glass/mouse (see below):

You can use a keyboard shortcut to enter or leave Print Preview: simply press Ctrl+Shift+B.

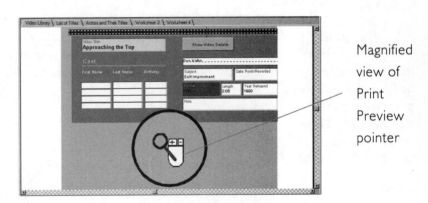

Magnified view of Print Preview pointer

Left-click once to zoom in (increase the magnification); right-click to zoom out (decrease the magnification).

Leaving Print Preview
Pull down the File menu and click Print Preview (the tick against the menu entry disappears).

Printing database data

You can print data from within forms or worksheets, in Browse or Design mode.

You can specify:

REMEMBER The available options differ slightly. For instance, in forms, you can choose which records you want printed *and/or* which pages; in worksheets, on the other hand, you can only specify pages.

- the number of copies you want printed

- whether you want the copies 'collated'. This is the process whereby Approach prints one full copy at a time. For instance, if you're printing four copies of a 20-page database, Approach prints pages 1-20 of the first copy, followed by pages 1-20 of the second and pages 1-20 of the third, etc.

- which pages or records (see the tip) you want printed

- the printer you want to use (if you have more than one installed on your system)

You can 'mix and match' these, as appropriate.

Starting a print run

HANDY TIP If you need to adjust your printer's internal settings before you initiate printing, click Properties. Then refer to your printer's manual.

Open the database/view which contains the data you want to print. Then pull down the File menu and click Print. Do any of steps 1-5 (3 and 4 are alternatives). Then carry out step 6 to begin printing:

1 Click here; choose a printer

6 Click here

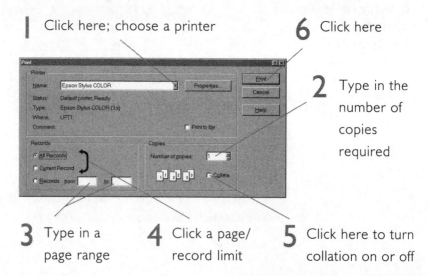

2 Type in the number of copies required

3 Type in a page range

4 Click a page/ record limit

5 Click here to turn collation on or off

Freelance Graphics

Use this chapter to acquire the basics of producing your own slide show. You'll learn how to use slide views to work with slides optimally, and how to apply new layouts to slides (complete with text, formatting and inserted pictures). Finally, you'll print out (optional) and run your presentation.

Covers

The Freelance Graphics screen

Below is a detailed illustration of the Freelance Graphics screen.

Title bar   Menu bar   Ruler

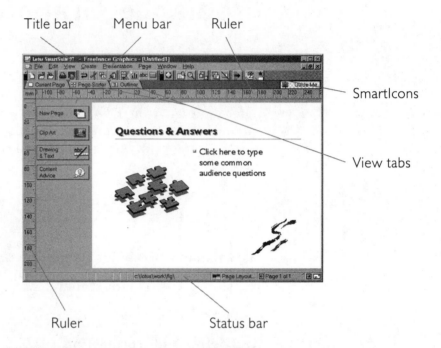

SmartIcons

View tabs

Ruler   Status bar

The rulers can be hidden, if required.

Showing/hiding the rulers

Pull down the View menu and click Set View Preferences.
Then do the following:

Deselect this

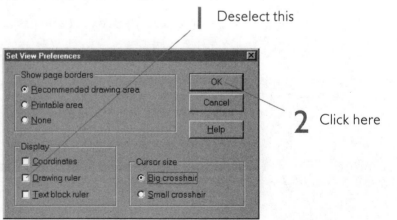

2 Click here

The slide views - an overview

Freelance Graphics has the following views:

Current Page   lets you work graphically with one page of your presentation

Outliner   shows the underlying textual structure of the presentation

Page Sorter   shows all the slides as icons, so you can manipulate them more easily

These are different ways of looking at and interacting with your presentation. The best way to work with presentations is to use a combination of all three, as appropriate.

Switching to a view

Pull down the View menu and click Current Page, Outliner or Page Sorter.

Excerpts from the three views are shown below:

Current Page View

Outliner View

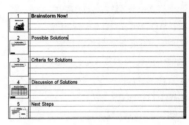

Page Sorter View

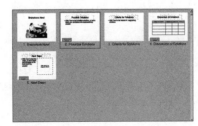

Using the slide views

The following are some brief supplemental notes on how best to use the Freelance Graphics views.

Current Page view

Current Page view displays the current slide in its own window. Use this view when you want a detailed picture of a slide – for instance, when you amend any of the slide contents (text or graphics), or when you change the overall formatting or add pages.

To switch from slide to slide, you can press Page Up or Page Down as appropriate. For more information on how to move around in presentations, see 'Moving through presentations' later.

Outliner view

If you're currently only working with the text in a given presentation, use Outliner view. Outliner view provides an overview of slide structure and content, together with icons representing slides visually.

When you delete a slide, Freelance Graphics does not provide a warning message: it's erased immediately. You can however reinstate it providing you press Ctrl+Z within 10 editing actions of the deletion.

Outliner has several useful features. For instance, you can opt to have text display with or without formatting (see page 137). You can also print out Outliner text – see the 'Printing' topic.

Page Sorter view

In Page Sorter view, slides display as thumbnails. You can perform useful actions on slides. First click a slide to select it (or select more than one by holding down the Shift key as you click them). Then:

To copy the slide(s)   click Duplicate Page in the Page menu

To delete the page(s)   press Delete

To change the size of the thumbnails uniformly, pull down the View menu and click Zoom, In (to increase the size) or Zoom, Out (to decrease it).

Restricting slide formatting

By default, Approach displays text formatting in Outliner view, and slides display as thumbnails. This means that all formatting enhancements to text display on screen as they would when printed (WYSIWYG – What You See Is What You Get). However, there are times when you won't want this.

In that case, you can:

- have slide thumbnails display in greyscales, rather than colour

- have slides display as text rather than thumbnails

- display text without formatting

Customising slide display

Pull down the View menu and do any of the following:

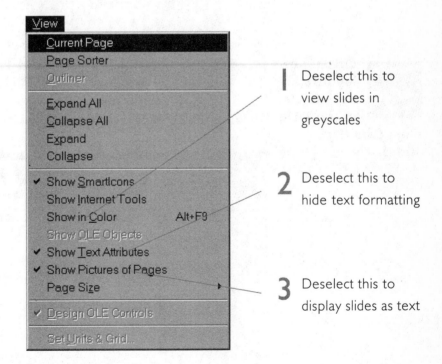

1 Deselect this to view slides in greyscales

2 Deselect this to hide text formatting

3 Deselect this to display slides as text

Customising slide structure

You can customise the basic format of slides very easily in Freelance Graphics by applying new SmartMasters globally. You can choose from over 100 SmartMaster layouts. When you've done this, you can then amend the individual components if you want (see later topics).

Applying a new layout

Make sure you're in Current Page or Page Sorter view. Pull down the Presentation menu and click Choose a Different SmartMaster Look. Then do the following:

1 Click a slide format

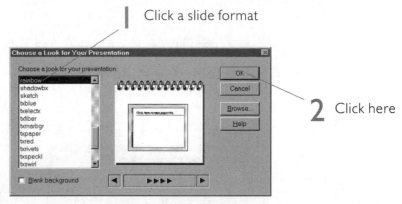

2 Click here

Often, new layouts are not visible in the Title page (the first slide).

The illustration below shows a slide with a new layout:

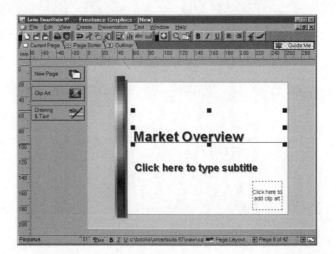

Adding text to slides

When you create a new slide show (unless you choose to create a blank presentation), Freelance Graphics fills each slide with placeholders containing sample text. The idea is that you should replace these with your own text.

The illustration below shows a sample slide before customisation:

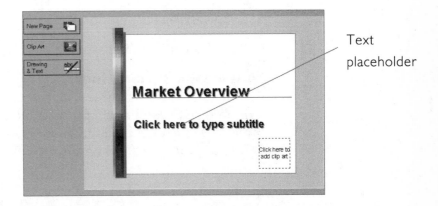

Text placeholder

To insert your own text, click in any text placeholder. Freelance Graphics displays a special text entry box. Now do the following:

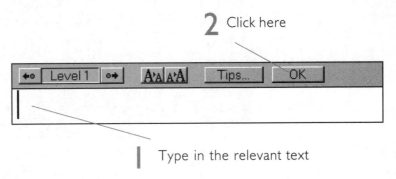

2 Click here

Type in the relevant text

Freelance Graphics inserts the new text.

Formatting text (1)

You can carry out a variety of formatting enhancements on text in slides. These include:

- changing the font and/or type size

- applying attributes

- applying a colour

- specifying the alignment

- specifying the line spacing

Font-based formatting

Double-click the relevant text object and select the text you want to format. Pull down the Text menu and click Text Properties. Carry out step 1 below. Then follow any of steps 2-6, as appropriate (if you follow step 5, also follow 6):

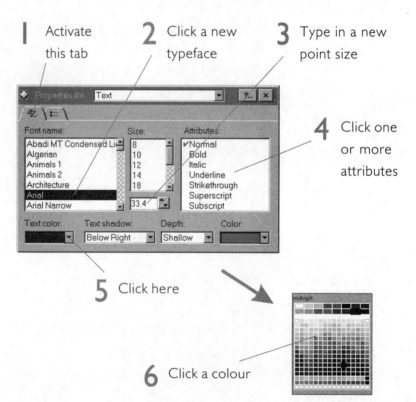

1 Activate this tab

2 Click a new typeface

3 Type in a new point size

4 Click one or more attributes

5 Click here

6 Click a colour

Formatting text (2)

Changing text spacing

First, click the relevant text object. Pull down the Text menu and click Text Properties. Carry out step 1 below. Now carry out steps 2-3, as appropriate:

| Activate this tab

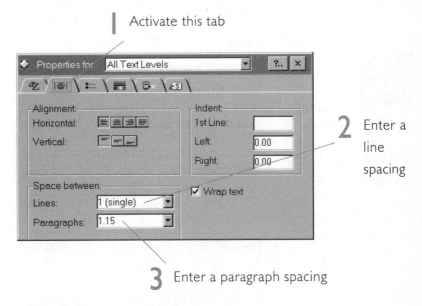

2 Enter a line spacing

3 Enter a paragraph spacing

Changing text alignment

First, click the relevant text object. Pull down the Text menu and do the following:

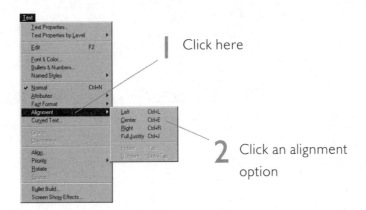

| Click here

2 Click an alignment option

Moving through presentations (1)

Since presentations – by their very nature – always have more than one slide, it's essential to be able to move from slide to slide easily (this is even more vital in the case of especially large presentations).

There are various methods you can use to move around in presentations – some work in all views, while others are limited to specific ones.

In Current Page view, the vertical scroll bar merely moves you around the slide currently being displayed.

Using the vertical scroll bar

In Page Sorter or Outliner views, move the mouse pointer over the vertical scroll box. Hold down the left mouse button and drag the box up or down to view other slides.

The illustration below shows the vertical scroll bar in use in Outliner view:

Scroll arrow

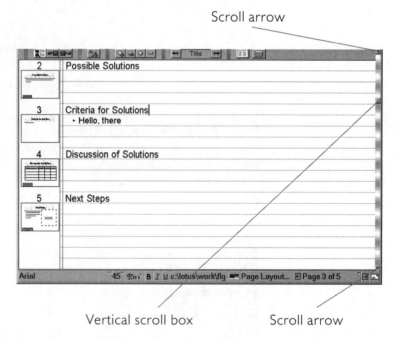

Vertical scroll box   Scroll arrow

Moving through presentations (2)

Using the Page Number box

Using the vertical scroll bar is a fairly inexact way to locate slides. A much more precise way is to use the Page Number box in the Status bar at the base of the screen.

Carry out steps 1 or 2, or 3&4 below:

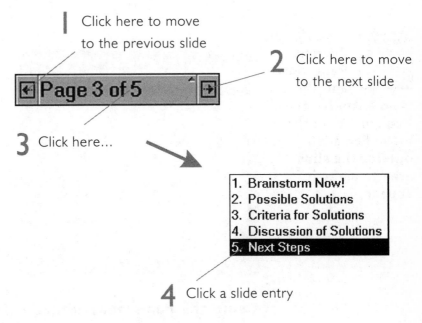

1 Click here to move to the previous slide

2 Click here to move to the next slide

3 Click here...

1. Brainstorm Now!
2. Possible Solutions
3. Criteria for Solutions
4. Discussion of Solutions
5. Next Steps

4 Click a slide entry

Using Page Sorter view

Page Sorter view offers a useful shortcut which you can use to jump immediately to a specific slide. Simply double-click any slide icon within Page Sorter view; Freelance Graphics then switches to Current Page view with the slide you selected displayed.

A selected slide in Page Sorter view; double-clicking this launches the slide in Current Page view

Moving through presentations (3)

Using the Go To Page dialog

You can use a dialog route from within any view to move to a specific slide.

Pull down the Page menu and click Go to Page. Now do the following:

If you're in Current Page view and there is no entry for the Page menu on the menu bar, click outside the slide area to make it appear.

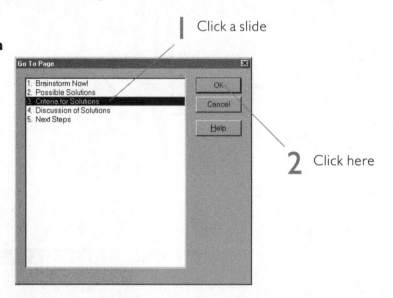

Click a slide

2 Click here

Using the Page menu directly

You can also use the Page menu itself (from within any view except Outliner) to move to the previous or next slide.

Pull down the Page menu and do the following:

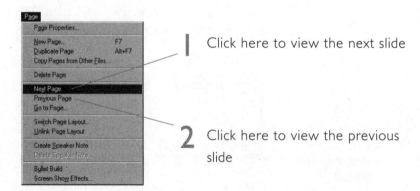

Click here to view the next slide

2 Click here to view the previous slide

Inserting & deleting slides

You'll often want to insert a slide within the body of a presentation. There are also occasions when you'll need to delete a slide because it's no longer required. Freelance Graphics lets you do both easily and conveniently.

If you add a new page in the Outliner view, you can only insert textual components; to add graphics etc., switch to Current Page view.

Inserting a slide

In any view, move to the slide which you want to precede the new one. Then pull down the Create menu and click Page.

Now do the following:

The current slide's Contents page is flagged (click another to apply a new one)

Re step 1 - if no Contents pages are associated with your presentation, click the Page Layouts tab instead, then select a layout for your new page. Finally, follow step 2.

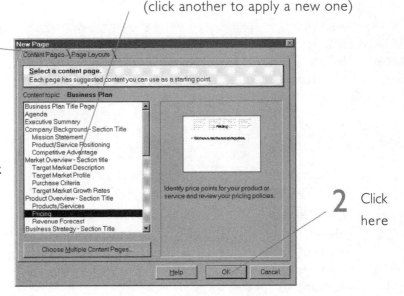

2 Click here

When you delete a slide, Freelance Graphics does not provide a message requiring your confirmation. The slide and its contents are erased immediately.

Deleting a slide

In Current Page view, move to the slide which you want to delete. In any other view, click it (or hold down one Shift key as you click on multiple slides to delete more than one). Then pull down the Page menu and click Delete Page.

Inserting pictures (1)

Pictures can help enormously in making your slide shows visually effective. You can add pictures in various ways.

Once inserted into a slide, pictures can be resized and moved in the normal way.

Adding clip art

You can add clip art contained in the SmartSuite Clip Art Gallery. The Gallery stores images in various categories.

In Current Page view, go to the slide into which you want the clip art added. Pull down the Create menu and click Add Clip Art. Now carry out the following steps:

You can also use this dialog to add diagrams. Click Diagram in the View section, then follow steps 1-3.

Click here; select a category from the list

3 Click here to add the picture to your slide

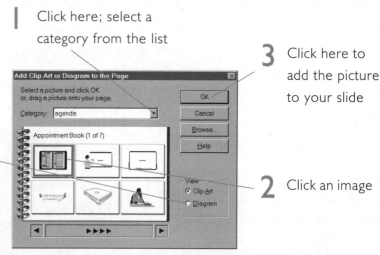

2 Click an image

Click ◀ to view earlier pictures, or ▶ to view later ones. (Doing this also steps through available categories.)

A slide with an added clip art image:

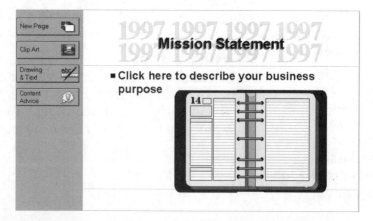

Inserting pictures (2)

Third party-images can be very useful in slides. They can be:

- output from other programs (e.g. drawings and illustrations)

- commercial clip art (e.g. bitmap images)

- photographs

Freelance Graphics will happily translate a wide variety of third-party graphics formats.

Adding a third-party picture

To insert a picture produced by another program, do the following. In Current Page view, go to the slide into which you want the picture added. Pull down the File menu and click Open. Now carry out the following steps:

Once inserted into a slide, pictures can be resized and moved in the normal way.

2 Click here. In the drop-down list, click the drive/folder that hosts the picture

After step 3, the following message appears:

Click Yes to store a full copy of the picture in your slide show, or No to insert a *linked* copy (this means that the graphic file must remain in its original location).

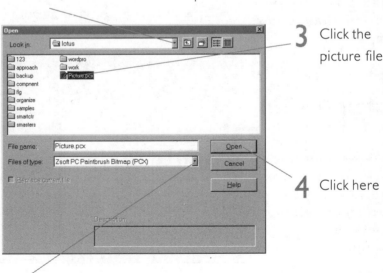

3 Click the picture file

4 Click here

| Click here; select a picture format from the list

Inserting pictures (3)

Freelance Graphics provides another technique for inserting pictures. Some slides come with graphics placeholders:

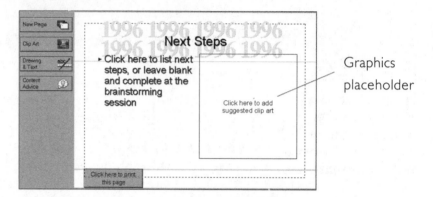

Graphics placeholder

HANDY TIP You can also use this dialog to add diagrams. Click Diagram in the View section, then follow steps 1-3.

Inserting pictures via placeholders

Click once within a graphic placeholder. Now do the following:

Click here; select a category from the list

HANDY TIP Click ◄ to view earlier pictures, or ► to view later ones. (Doing this also steps through available categories.)

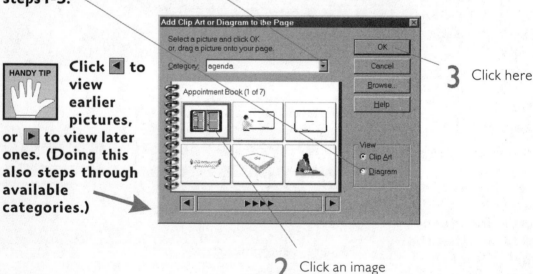

3 Click here

2 Click an image

Print Preview (1)

Freelance Graphics provides a further view called Print Preview. Print Preview can be launched from within any other slide view, and indicates what your presentation will look like when printed out (you might need to do this for a variety of reasons, for instance if you supply handouts with your slide show).

Print Preview displays one full page at a time (even if you eventually opt to print more than one slide on each page).

Launching Print Preview

If you're using the Page Sorter or Outliner views, select the slide you want to preview. If you're using Current Page view, go to the relevant slide. In either case, now pull down the File menu and carry out step 1, followed by 2 or 3. Finally, carry out step 4.

 If you're using a black-and-white printer, Print Preview displays your slides as greyscale images; if you're using a colour printer, on the other hand, they display in colour.

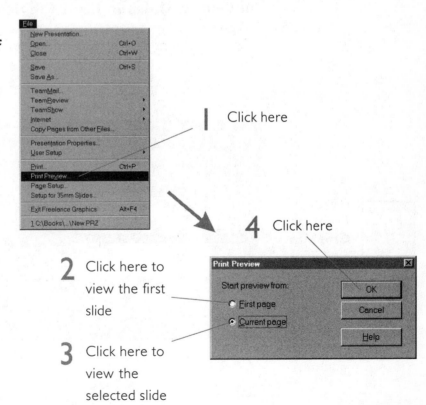

Click here

2 Click here to view the first slide

3 Click here to view the selected slide

4 Click here

Print Preview (2)

Using Print Preview
Your slide in Print Preview will look something like this:

To leave Print Preview and return to your slide show, click: Quit

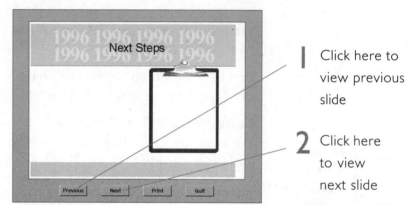

1 Click here to view previous slide

2 Click here to view next slide

Moving to slides in Print Preview
Follow steps 1 or 2 above to view adjacent slides.
Alternatively, press Esc then do the following:

1 Click a slide

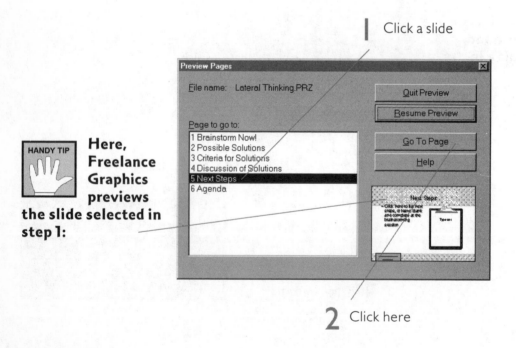

Here, Freelance Graphics previews the slide selected in step 1:

2 Click here

Printing - an overview

Freelance Graphics makes printing easy. You can specify:

- which pages are printed (you can specify a range – e.g. 3-12 – or print the whole of a presentation)

- the number of copies

- whether you want the copies 'collated' (one full copy printed at a time). For instance, if you're printing three copies of a 10-page presentation, SmartSuite prints pages 1-10 inclusive of the first version, followed by pages 1-10 of the second and pages 1-10 of the third

- the print orientation:

 Portrait

 Landscape

- whether printing is (in effect) in 'Draft' (Freelance Graphics prints no background layouts, and the print time is therefore reduced)

- whether Freelance Graphics prints your text outline (this option is only available from within the Outliner view)

- whether your presentation should be printed as a handout, with more than one slide on each page

- whether handouts should be printed with blank lines, for annotation ('Audience Notes')

- which printer you use

Printing a presentation

If you want to print out your presentation's outline, first make sure you're in Outliner view.

Pull down the File menu and click Print. Now carry out any of steps 1-6 below, as appropriate (if you follow step 6, also carry out 7 and 8). Finally, follow step 9.

HANDY TIP

Re step 4 - if you click an option apart from Full Page or Outline, select a layout in this section:

HANDY TIP

To print in Draft, click the Options button, then here:

Finally, click here, then follow the other steps in the main illustration, as appropriate.

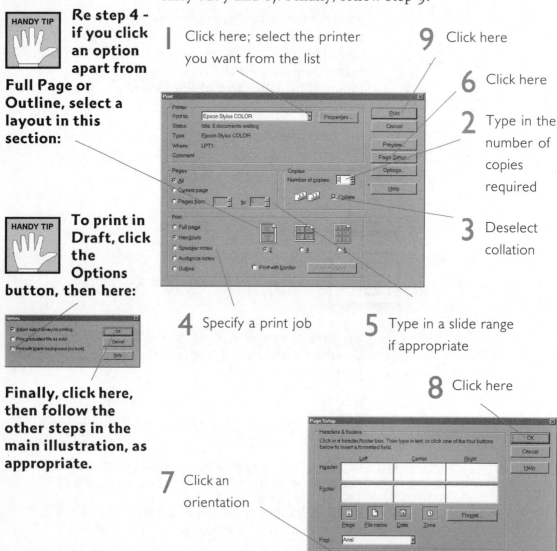

1 Click here; select the printer you want from the list

9 Click here

6 Click here

2 Type in the number of copies required

3 Deselect collation

4 Specify a print job

5 Type in a slide range if appropriate

8 Click here

7 Click an orientation

Running a presentation (1)

Once you've created (and possibly printed) your slide show, it's time to run it. Before you do so, however, you should set the run parameters.

When you run your presentation you can, if you want, have Freelance Graphics wait for your command before moving from slide to slide. This is useful if you anticipate being interrupted during the presentation. You retain full control over delivery. Alternatively, you can have the slide show run automatically.

You can also specify a common transition effect. Transition effects make the intervals between slides more dramatic, and therefore enhance the overall visual impact of your presentations.

HANDY TIP

Before you actually run your slide show, it's a good idea to 'rehearse' it. This is a dummy run during which you can verify whether the presentation is performing as it should; if it isn't, you can correct it on-the-fly. (See 'Running a Presentation (2)'.)

Preparing to run your slide show
First, open the presentation you want to run. Then (in any view except Outliner) pull down the Presentation menu and click Set Up Screen Show. Now follow steps 1-5 below, as appropriate:

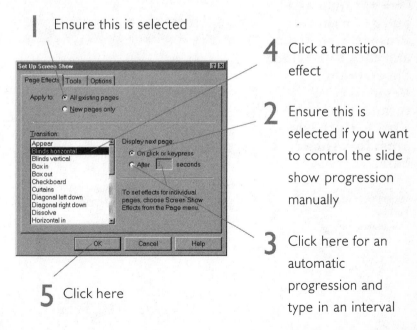

1 Ensure this is selected

4 Click a transition effect

2 Ensure this is selected if you want to control the slide show progression manually

3 Click here for an automatic progression and type in an interval

5 Click here

Running a presentation (2)

This message appears because (on page 153) you've already allocated slide intervals.

Rehearsing your presentation

In any view, pull down the Presentation menu and click Rehearse, Start. Do the following:

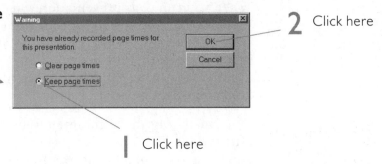

2 Click here

Click here

Freelance Graphics now launches the first slide of your presentation. At the bottom of the screen is the timer. Do the following:

To run your slide show after rehearsal, pull down the Presentation menu and click Run Screen Show, From Beginning. To terminate a show before it's finished, press Esc. Then click here:

Click here; the timer counts the interval until the next slide. When the timing is right, follow steps 2 and 3

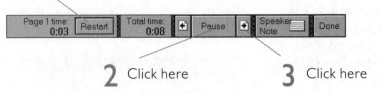

2 Click here   **3** Click here

After step 3, Freelance Graphics moves to the next slide. Repeat steps 1-3 until all the slides have had intervals allocated. Finally, another dialog appears:

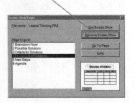

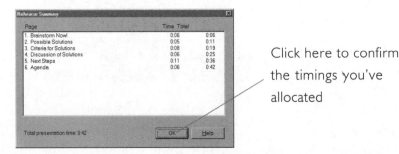

Click here to confirm the timings you've allocated

Index